SQUASH

Steps to Success

Philip Yarrow
Dunlop/Slazenger National Advisory Staff

Human Kinetics

Library of Congress Cataloging-in-Publication Data

Yarrow, Philip, 1968-
    Squash : steps to success / Philip Yarrow.
      p.   cm. -- (Steps to success)
    ISBN 0-88011-541-6
    1. Squash rackets (Game) I. Title. II. Series: Steps to success
activity series.
    GV1004.Y37   1997
    796.343--dc21   97-10150
                                         CIP

ISBN-10: 0-88011-541-6
ISBN-13: 978-0-88011-541-4

Acquisitions Editor: Kenneth Mange; **Developmental Editor:** Judy Patterson Wright, PhD; **Assistant Editors**: Andrew Smith and Jacqueline Eaton Blakley; **Editorial Assistant:** Jennifer Jeanne Hemphill; **Copyeditor:** Bob Replinger; **Proofreader:** Erin Cler; **Graphic Designer:** Keith Blomberg; **Graphic Artist:** Denise Lowry; **Cover Designer:** Jack Davis; **Cover Photograph:** Wilmer Zehr; **Illustrators:** Matthew Hutton and Dianna Porter; **Printer:** United Graphics

Instructional Designer for the Steps to Success Activity Series: Joan N. Vickers, EdD, University of Calgary, Calgary, Alberta, Canada

Human Kinetics books are available at special discounts for bulk purchase. Special editions or book excerpts can also be created to specification. For details, contact the Special Sales Manager at Human Kinetics.

Printed in the United States of America   15   14

Human Kinetics
Web site: www.HumanKinetics.com

United States: Human Kinetics, P.O. Box 5076, Champaign, IL 61825-5076
800-747-4457
e-mail: humank@hkusa.com

Canada: Human Kinetics, 475 Devonshire Road, Unit 100, Windsor, ON N8Y 2L5
800-465-7301 (in Canada only)
e-mail: orders@hkcanada.com

Europe: Human Kinetics, 107 Bradford Road, Stanningley
Leeds LS28 6AT, United Kingdom
+44 (0) 113 255 5665
e-mail: hk@hkeurope.com

Australia: Human Kinetics, 57A Price Avenue, Lower Mitcham, South Australia 5062
08 8372 0999
e-mail: liaw@hkaustralia.com

New Zealand: Human Kinetics, Division of Sports Distributors NZ Ltd.
P.O. Box 300 226 Albany, North Shore City, Auckland
0064 9 448 1207
e-mail: info@humankinetics.co.nz

Contents

PREFACE

Squash is one of the world's fastest growing sports. The physical and mental demands make it one of the most satisfying sports to play. It takes just minutes to learn, yet a lifetime to master. To play squash well demands a combination of practice, patience, and instruction. The objective of this book is to provide you with instruction that will make your practice and patience pay off.

Squash: Steps to Success has 12 steps that help you develop the basic skills and ideas, and then incorporate them into match play. A series of drills appears at the end of each step, designed to help you practice the skills and ideas discussed in the step. The drills are ordered so that you can first practice the skill or topic in isolation, then under more pressure, and finally in a gamelike situation. Each step has a mixture of four types of drills:

- *Solo practices*—the skill or topic is practiced in isolation through continuous repetition.
- *Hitting from a partner's feed*—the skill or topic is practiced under more pressure. Your partner's feed will usually be a racket feed to a certain area of the court. Some drills require your partner to throw the ball. Occasionally, a drill of this type may use two feeders.
- *Two- or three-person routines*—the skill or idea is practiced in a drill that will simulate a game. These drills are designed to be continuous. You should be able to keep the drill going without having to stop to pick up the ball.
- *Conditioned games*—the skill or idea is practiced in a modified game situation; you can use only certain shots or a certain area of the court.

Each of the drills includes suggestions for increasing or decreasing the difficulty so you can progress at your own pace.

The sequence of the steps has been carefully developed to help you quickly achieve a solid squash game built on sound fundamentals. The first five steps teach you the basics of swinging and moving around the court. The next five steps outline the specific strokes necessary for a solid basic game. The first of these steps, the volley, introduces you to hitting the ball out of the air. You are then ready to concentrate on two of the most important aspects of the game—the serve and return of serve. The final steps introduce more advanced topics and summarize the basic strategies involved in squash.

Progress through the steps as fast or as slow as you like, but remember that to become a good squash player you must develop a strong basic swing and correct court movement. The early steps are the backbone to your squash game and will provide you with the strength to develop rapidly and achieve satisfaction as a player.

I would like to thank my wife, Virginia, for all her help with the countless rough drafts of this book. Also, I would like to thank Katherine Johnson, Beau River, Imran Nasir, Tim Long, and Gus Cook for modeling for the illustrations.

THE STEPS TO SUCCESS STAIRCASE

Get ready to climb a staircase—one that will lead you to become an accomplished squash player. You can't leap to the top; you get there by climbing one step at a time.

Each of the 12 steps you will take is an easy transition from the one before. The first few steps of the staircase provide a solid foundation of basic skills and ideas. As you progress, you'll learn how to develop these skills and ideas to maneuver your opponent around the squash court. As you near the top of the staircase, you'll become more confident in your ability to challenge higher-level players in league or tournament play or just for fun.

Read this section, as well as "The Game Of Squash" and "Selecting Your Equipment" sections, for an orientation and help with setting up your practice sessions around the steps.

Follow the same sequence each step (chapter) of the way:

1. Read the explanations of what the step covers, why the step is important, and how to execute or perform the step's focus, which may be on basic skills, ideas, tactics, or a combination of the three.
2. Follow the numbered illustrations showing exactly how to position your body to execute each basic skill. Each skill has three general parts: preparation (getting into a starting position), execution (performing the skill that is the focus of the step), and follow-through (reaching a finish position or following through to starting position).
3. Look over the common errors that may occur and the recommendations for how to correct them.
4. The drills help you improve your skills through repetition and purposeful practice. Read the directions and the Success Goal for each drill. Practice accordingly and record your scores. Compare your score with the Success Goal for the drill. You need to meet the Success Goal of each drill before moving on to practice the next one because the drills are arranged in an easy-to-difficult progression. This sequence is designed to help you achieve continual success.
5. When you can reach all the Success Goals for one step, you are ready for a qualified observer—such as your teacher, coach, or trained partner—to evaluate your basic skill technique against the Keys to Success checklist. This is a qualitative or subjective evaluation of your basic technique or form, because using correct form can enhance your performance.
6. Repeat these procedures for each of the 12 Steps to Success. Then rate yourself according to the directions in the "Rating Your Progress" section.

Good luck on your step-by-step journey to developing your squash skills, building confidence, experiencing success, and having fun!

Key

→ path of player

········→ ball path of player A

– – – – → ball path of player B

– – – – → ball path of player C

A, B, C = players

■ object on floor

THE GAME OF SQUASH

Not enough time in your life to play a sport regularly? Do you only have time in your schedule to do a boring, repetitive workout that lacks competition and mental stimulation. Think again! Playing squash develops speed, endurance, agility, coordination, and court savvy, yet the average length of a match between two recreational players is just 40 minutes! Squash is one of the fastest and most athletic sports. The popularity of the sport is due in large part to the intensely competitive workout it generates in such a short time. It's the perfect sport for busy people. Over 15 million men and women in 122 nations now enjoy squash, and the numbers are increasing rapidly.

The beauty of the game is that it's simple to learn yet difficult to master. All you do is hit a small ball against the front wall of a room so that it is out of reach of your opponent. The challenge, of course, is achieving this goal against the more skilled opponents you'll play as you improve. The game can be physically and mentally torturous, but at the end of the match you'll be satisfied, exhilarated, and possibly a little tired!

History of Squash

People have been playing games for centuries that involve hitting a ball with a racket, either against a wall or back and forth to each other across a net. The most common example is tennis. In the 19th century the popularity of sports involving rackets and balls led to the creation of the game *rackets* in the Fleet Prison in London, England. The prisoners exercised by hitting a small, hard ball around the walls of a large room. Ironically, the game later became popular in English public schools.

It was at one of these schools, Harrow School in London, where squash is believed to have originated around 1830. Students, waiting to get on to the rackets court, began practicing in a smaller area by hitting a soft rubber ball against the wall. They found that playing with the softer ball produced a wider variety of shots and required much greater effort. The name of the game came from the ball's "squashiness" as it hit the walls.

In the early years of the sport there was little standardization. Many slight variations of the game were seen. Fortunately, only two variations became popular. Most of the world played with a "soft" ball on 21-foot-wide courts, while North Americans played with a "hard" ball on slightly narrower courts.

The rules of the "soft ball" version of the game were finally formalized in 1923, and the number of squash players soon overtook its parent game, rackets. The growth areas for squash at this time were in countries where British forces were stationed. People in India, Pakistan, Egypt, South Africa, Australia, and New Zealand began to learn the game. In 1930, the first British Open was held, and it was considered the first unofficial World Championships. An Englishman, Don Butcher, won the event, beating fellow Englishman

Charles Read in a best-of-three match series. For the following 35 years players from Egypt and Pakistan dominated top-level squash. Many of these players learned the game as ball boys for uncovered courts. They had limited coaching but plenty of time to practice. They developed techniques that involved exotic shot making and became extremely proficient at the game.

In the late 1960s Jonah Barrington, a rugged, determined Irishman, finally broke the Egyptian and Pakistani domination. Barrington didn't begin playing squash until his early 20s, but he showed an unparalleled dedication to the game. His rigorous training took him to a fitness level far above that of the top players of the day. Barrington won the British Open six times, proving that fitness could prevail over shot making.

Squash would never be the same again. Barrington pushed all the top professionals to work hard on their fitness. The players that have followed in Barrington's footsteps all possessed remarkable speed, stamina, and strength besides incredible racket skills. Three players stand out: Australia's Geoff Hunt, and Pakistan's Jahangir Khan and Jansher Khan. Hunt was the best of a number of strong players who emerged in the 1970s from Australia. He took over from Barrington as the number-one player in the world. Jahangir Khan is widely regarded as the greatest ever to play the game. His aggressive style overwhelmed opponents. He was so dominant that at one stage, during the 1980s, he went five and a half years without losing a single match. Jansher Khan, no relation to Jahangir, was finally able to combat Jahangir's strength by skillfully varying the pace of matches. Jansher is currently the top player in the world but is chased by a host of young players, predominantly from Australia and Britain.

In North America the squash scene has changed rapidly over the past few years. Squash, as most of the world knows it, was played in North America only recreationally in the summertime. In the winter tournament season, the exclusively North American game known as hard-ball squash, played on narrower courts with a hard, solid ball, was the sole game. Recently, though, the popularity of the international soft-ball version of the game has spread rapidly. Most players now play soft-ball exclusively, throughout the year. The two games require different techniques and strategies. The hard ball travels faster around the court and thus requires quicker reflexes. The rallies tend to be short, and the ability to hit winners is essential. The soft ball also travels at high speeds but slows as it rebounds off the walls and floor. The players must run more but they have more time to play their shots. Winning shots are harder to come by in soft-ball. Rallies are longer, and to win points a player must use a combination of shots to work the opponent out of position. These differences have made the conversion from the hard-ball game difficult for many long-time squash enthusiasts in North America. The problem is compounded by the lack of experienced soft-ball coaches to help these players make the necessary changes to their games. This book focuses exclusively on the soft-ball version of the game.

Despite its ever growing popularity around the world, squash has suffered from underexposure because of the difficulty in viewing games. In the past, spectators could see matches only from balconies above the back wall of the court, severely restricting their number. In the 1970s, however, glass back walls were introduced, soon followed by fully transparent portable courts for major events, with special one-way-view perspex walls. These courts can be erected in large halls, allowing spectators to be seated around the court and to watch from all angles. Audiences of over three thousand people can now attend these events.

Still, with two players hitting a small, fast-moving ball in an enclosed room, squash has proved to be an extremely difficult sport to televise. Recent innovations in this area, however, have opened up opportunities. Besides the perspex courts, which allow a variety of camera angles, colored walls and specially constructed balls have helped make television viewing easier. White balls were used first, followed by balls with reflective dots on the surface that caused the ball to glow in the presence of an ultraviolet light. These improvements, along with a new generation of high-definition television cameras, have made the ball easier to follow on a television screen. These developments may allow greater exposure for the sport in the future.

Playing a Match

Squash is played by two people on a court 32 feet long and 21 feet wide (see figure 1). After a five-minute warm-up, the players decide who will serve first by spinning a racket. The ball is put into play by a serve, and a rally is played out. A player wins a rally when the opponent either hits the ball into the tin (a metal strip 19 inches high at the bottom of the front wall), hits above the out lines, or doesn't reach the ball before it bounces twice. During the rally the player may hit the ball on the fly or after it has hit the floor and may

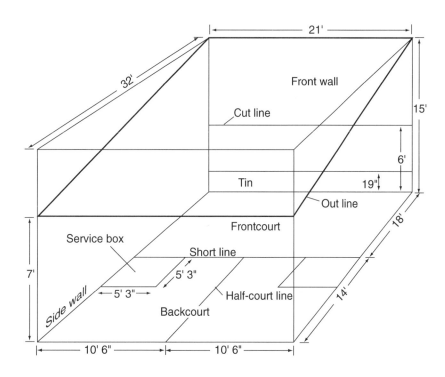

Figure 1 Court markings and dimensions.

use the side and back walls to maneuver the ball onto the front wall.

Most squash matches use the "traditional" (or "International") scoring system, in which a player scores points only when serving, and each game is played to 9 points. In the past few years, however, professional tournaments have begun to use "point-per-rally" (or "American") scoring, in which a player winning the rally scores a point regardless of who served. In point-per-rally scoring each game is played to 15 points. This scoring system was introduced due to the increasing length of matches in professional tournaments. Many matches would last well over two hours because the score wouldn't change for long periods while the players traded serves. Even with the point-per-rally scoring, rallies and games in professional matches can last a long time, but seldom more than two hours.

Normally a player wins a match by winning three out of five games. Occasionally, matches are won by winning two out of three games.

A match can also involve two teams of players. Each team normally consists of three or five players. The top players on each team (known as first string) play each other, the second-best players (second string) play each other, and so on down the team. A team scores a point for each match won.

A tournament involves a number of players or teams competing against each other. Most tournaments are single elimination—a player or team losing a match is eliminated from the tournament. Some tournaments, however, are double elimination. A player or team must lose twice before being eliminated. Another kind of tournament is the round-robin tournament, in which the player or team plays all the other players or teams in the tournament. The winner of the tournament is the player or team recording the most wins.

Squash Rules

When the players step on court they have five minutes to warm up before the first game begins. During the warm-up the players stand on opposite sides of the court and hit the ball against the front wall so that it rebounds to their opponent. After two and a half minutes of the warm-up the players switch sides of the court. The warm-up serves two purposes: It gives the players an opportunity to practice their strokes, and it allows them to warm up the ball. A squash ball is cold at first and doesn't bounce much. Once the players begin to hit it, the ball becomes warmer and begins to bounce more. The ball should be warm before the players start the first game.

After the warm-up the players spin a racket to decide who will serve first. The winner of the racket spin may elect to serve or receive. Nearly always the player will choose to serve, particularly with traditional scoring in which a player can score only when serving.

Service

The player serving first can decide whether to serve from the left or right service box. Normally, players serve from the right service box against right-handed opponents and from the left service box against left-handed opponents. They do this so they can serve to their opponent's backhand side, which is often the weaker side.

The server must have at least one foot inside the service box when contacting the ball. Part of the foot can be off the floor, but none of the foot can be touching any of the lines forming the service box.

The server throws the ball in the air and hits it before it hits the floor, directly onto the front wall. The ball must strike the front wall above the cut line and below the out line. It must then rebound to the opposite back quarter of the court. If the receiver hits the ball on the fly (that is, before it bounces on the floor), the serve is good. If, however, the receiver allows the ball to bounce before hitting it, the ball must bounce within the back quarter of the court for the serve to be good. The opposite back quarter is the area enclosed by the short line, half-court line, side wall, and back wall, on the opposite side of the court from the service box the server served from. (Note: Hitting the short line or the half-court line isn't considered a good serve.) The ball may hit the side wall, the back wall, or both walls before striking the floor as long as it strikes the walls below the out line. An unsuccessful service is called a fault, and the receiver immediately wins the rally. The following is a complete list of all possible types of faults:

- Server doesn't have at least one foot in the service box at point of contact *(foot fault)*.
- Server hits the ball after it hits the floor.
- Server swings and misses the ball.
- Ball fails to hit the front wall above the cut line.
- Ball hits one of the side walls before hitting the front wall.
- Ball bounces outside the opposite back quarter of the court.
- Ball hits front, side, or back wall above the out line.
- Server hits the ball twice.
- Server is struck with the ball after it rebounds from the front wall.

Winning a Rally

Once the server has completed the service, the cut line and all the lines on the floor play no further part in the rally. The only boundaries now are the out lines and the tin.

Besides winning a rally when your opponent is unsuccessful with a serve, you win a rally if your opponent

- fails to hit the ball before it bounces twice,
- fails to hit the ball against the front wall,
- hits the ball into the tin,
- hits the ball onto the floor before it hits the front wall,
- hits the ball onto any of the walls on or above the out line,
- hits the ball onto the ceiling or against or through any fittings hanging from the ceiling,
- carries the ball on the racket strings or hits the ball twice,
- touches the ball with anything other than the racket,
- deliberately interferes with your shot, or
- accidentally interferes with your shot to such an extent that you're impeded from making a possible winning shot (discussed further in the lets and strokes segment of this section).

Scoring

Most squash matches are scored with the traditional scoring system in which games are played to 9 points and points are scored only by the server. If the receiver wins the rally the score doesn't change, but the receiver gains the serve for the next rally. When the score is called out, the server's points are always called first. For example the score 3-5 means the server has 3 points and the receiver 5 points. If both players have the same number of points, for example 3-3, the score is called as "3 all." If a player has 0 points the term *love* is used. Therefore, at the beginning of each game the score is "love all."

If the game score reaches 8-8, a tie break is used. The player who reaches 8 points first will be the receiver and chooses either *set one* to play the game to 9 points, or *set two* to play the game to 10 points. Usually the receiver will choose set two, because choosing set one immediately gives the server *game ball*, meaning the player is one rally away from winning the game, or match ball—the player is one rally from winning the match.

As mentioned earlier, professional tournaments have recently begun to use point-per-rally scoring. Each game is played to 15 points, and points are scored regardless of which player served. Point-per-rally tie breaks occur when the score reaches 14-14. The receiver now has the choice of either *set one* or *set three* and the game is played to 15 or 17, respectively. The best strategy for the receiver isn't so clear now. Choosing set one still gives the server game ball, but because either player can score a point by winning the next rally, the receiver has game ball as well. Most players consider set three the safest option, but it all depends on your gut feeling of your chances of winning the next rally.

Safety

Two players moving rapidly around a small room have a high risk of injury from running into each other or hitting each other with the ball or racket. For this reason both players must always be aware of the position of their opponent. The responsibility for safety during a rally lies with both the striker (the player about to hit the ball) and the nonstriker (the player who has just hit the ball). The nonstriker should make sure the striker has a direct line to move to the ball and has room to make a full swing at the ball. Crowding your opponent is not only hazardous to your health but also unsportsmanlike. When striking the ball you should be aware of exactly where your opponent is so that you minimize the risk of injuring your opponent with the racket or the ball. Think about trying to control your racket as you swing; avoid particularly an excessive follow-through. If you feel there is the possibility of hitting your opponent with either your racket or the ball, stop and ask for a *let* (that is, for the rally to be replayed).

One of the most dangerous situations that can occur is when you turn on the ball. This is when you are in a back corner and the ball bounces off the side wall and the back wall out toward the center of the court. Instead of backing up toward the center of the court to allow room to hit the ball, you make a 180-degree turn and hit the ball on the opposite side of your body. This is dangerous because as you turn you can't see your opponent. Your opponent has no idea where you're going to hit the ball and doesn't know where to move to avoid being hit. If this situation occurs *always* stop before hitting the ball and request a let.

Lets and Strokes

To promote safety in a match the rules provide for a system of *lets* and *strokes*. This complex system includes many gray areas concerning whether a let or a stroke (penalty point) should be awarded.

In considering lets and strokes, you should keep two main points in mind: safety and fairness. Safety is of prime importance. If a player discontinues playing a shot because of a genuine concern about hitting an opponent, the player is entitled to at least a let as long as he or she could have made a good return. Beginners often start off playing lets whenever there is any interference. This certainly increases safety. But you should consider what is fair as well. Sometimes the player that has stopped has such a clear advantage that he or she would almost certainly have won the rally if not for the interference of the opponent. Often, the opponent has made every effort to avoid the interference, but it was caused by his or her own poor shot. In this situation the opponent deserves to lose the rally. So when a player stops, the hypothetically fair outcome should be considered. If a player who clearly had the upper hand stops because the opponent was in the way, the fair outcome is to award a stroke.

To give you a greater understanding of the rules regarding lets and strokes, we'll consider three common occurrences on a squash court. While reading the following remember two things: If your opponent's actions were a deliberate act to interfere with your shot, you're always entitled to a stroke; and if you wouldn't have been able to make a good return, the decision should always be a *no let* (that is, you lose the rally).

Hitting Your Opponent With the Ball

The rules state that once your opponent has struck the ball, you must have the entire front wall to aim at. Therefore, if you hit your opponent with the ball the decision about whether to award a let or a stroke depends on whether the ball was traveling directly toward the front wall. If it was, you are entitled to a stroke because your opponent failed to give you the whole of the front wall to aim at. If the ball was traveling toward the side wall (or back wall), a let should be played.

Deliberately striking your opponent with the ball is dangerous and unsportsmanlike. If you're in a situation where you think you may strike your opponent, you should refrain from hitting the ball. The rules apply in exactly the same way. If you would have struck your opponent with a shot going directly toward the front wall, you're entitled to a stroke. If you would have struck your opponent with a shot going toward the side (or back) wall, the decision is a let.

The only exception to these rules is if you turn on the ball. Under no circumstance can you be awarded a stroke if you turn on the ball, regardless of whether you hit your opponent or would have hit your opponent with a shot traveling directly toward the front wall. Whenever you're in a situation where you have turned on the ball, you should stop and a let should be played. *Turned on the ball* refers not only to when you make a 180-degree turn in the back corner but also to when you allow the ball to travel around your back or when you hit the ball between your legs or behind your back.

Your Opponent Impedes You From Reaching the Ball

The rules state that your opponent, after striking the ball, must give you direct access to the ball. If your opponent impedes your direct access to the ball, the decision about whether to award a let or a stroke depends on whether you were stopped from playing a possible winning shot. So it depends largely on how good your opponent's shot was. If it was a good shot and you would have only been able to keep the ball in play, you're entitled to a let. If it was a poor shot and you would have had a good opportunity to hit a winner, you're entitled to a stroke.

The rules also state that you must make every effort to reach the ball. This prevents you from claiming a let at the slightest sign of interference when you see that your opponent has hit a good shot or when you're too tired to run for the ball. However, you don't have to crash full speed into your opponent to claim a let. You should stop before making significant contact.

Your Opponent Doesn't Give You Enough Room to Swing at the Ball

The rules state that your opponent must give you complete freedom to play any shot you choose. If your opponent crowds you and inhibits your backswing or your follow-through, you're entitled to a stroke as long as you could have played a shot directly to the front wall. If you could have hit a shot only to the side or back walls, you're entitled to a let only.

Besides being awarded for interference, lets are also awarded in these situations:

■ If the ball breaks or splits during a rally

■ If the receiver isn't ready and makes no attempt to hit a service
■ If there is a distraction on or off court

Roles of the Marker and Referee

In top-level events, two people—a marker and a referee—normally officiate matches. The *marker* is responsible for

■ announcing the match to the spectators,
■ calling the score,
■ calling service faults, down (the ball hitting the tin), out, and not up (the ball bounces twice or is struck twice), and
■ repeating decisions made by the referee.

The *referee* is responsible for

■ making decisions on appeals for lets,
■ making decisions on appeals against the marker's calls,
■ correcting any errors made by the marker (for example, with the score), and
■ keeping track of the time during the warm-up and between games. (Note that players are allowed a 90-second break between games.)

Sometimes a single official will perform the duties of both the referee and the marker. Probably more often, however, you must officiate your own matches. In this situation the server should call out the score before serving to reduce the chances of a conflict over the score. The players must agree about whether interference warrants a let or a stroke. This can lead to many disputes, which more often than not will mean playing a let. You should remember, however, that not offering your opponent a stroke when you know one is deserved or taking a let when you couldn't have made a good return is cheating!

If you feel you deserve a let or a stroke, you should appeal to the referee (or to your opponent if you have no referee). The correct way to appeal is to call out "let please." You should never ask for a stroke. The referee (or you and your opponent mutually) will decide the correct award. You should remember that you must appeal at the time of the incident. Appealing a few shots later or at the end of the rally about interference or some kind of distraction isn't permitted. It will be considered that you played through the interference, and you won't be awarded a let.

This limited interpretation of the rules is a good basis from which to start. As you become a more experienced player, particularly if you begin to play in tournaments, you must study the rules in greater depth.[1]

Warming Up and Cooling Down

Because squash is physically demanding, you must prepare properly before the start of a match to reduce the chances of injury. A pregame warm-up should last for 15 to 20 minutes and should include a "pulse warmer" to increase the heart rate, some slow stretching, and some mobility exercises.

---

[1] A good book to help players learn the rules in more depth is *Squash Rules For Players* by Rod Symington, available from the United States Squash Racquets Association, P.O. Box 1216, Bala-Cynwyd, PA 19004.

Do some jogging or skipping as your pulse warmer. This will warm up the muscles and get the blood circulating faster. By warming up your muscles you'll reduce the risk of pulling a muscle while stretching, and the stretching will be more effective. Slow stretching should include exercises for the calf, hamstrings, quadriceps, adductors, and hip flexors. Hold the stretches for a count of 10 seconds and repeat at least three times. The mobilizing exercises (such as arm circles, trunk twists, or knee bends) are free brisk exercises to mobilize the joints of the shoulders, legs, and trunk. Perform each joint mobilizer 10 to 20 times.

You're now ready to begin the five-minute on-court warm-up period. Use this time to groove your shots and take a look at your opponent. It can be dangerous to read too much into your opponent's warm-up, but you may be able to get an idea about how he or she will play. For example, you may be able to determine whether your opponent is a hard hitter or a volleyer.

The cooling-down period at the end of the match is just as important as the warm-up. You should avoid sitting down immediately after you have finished because your muscles will begin to tighten up and you'll feel very sore the next day! Instead, take time to go through some slow stretching exercises and some gentle jogging before heading for the shower.

Getting Started

Now that you have a little background on the game, all you need to do is find a court. In the United States, squash traditionally was played mainly by wealthy men in private men's clubs. Recently, however, a number of people have switched from playing racquetball to playing squash. This has spurred many health-club owners to convert racquetball courts to squash courts or to build squash courts in new complexes. The converted racquetball courts are one foot narrower than official international standards but have opened up the game to a wider variety of people. Besides health clubs, many universities and some YMCAs have courts. Most cities in the United States have some squash courts, and the numbers are increasing.

If you're not sure where you can play in your area, contact the United States Squash Racquets Association (USSRA), the governing body for squash in the United States:

United States Squash Racquets Association
P.O. Box 1216
Bala-Cynwyd, PA 19004
Tel: 610-667-4006
Fax: 610-667-6539

ELECTING YOUR EQUIPMENT

You can buy squash equipment from most major sports stores or from the pro shop at your squash club.

Rackets

Squash rackets range in price from $30 to $180. The important aspects to consider when choosing a racket are weight, racket-head size, and stiffness. Beginners who don't want to spend too much money on a racket should be able to find a suitable racket at the lower end of that price range. As you play more you may find that a more expensive racket improves your game.

A squash racket is similar to a racquetball racket except that it has a longer shaft (see figure 2). Until the early 1980s most squash rackets were made of wood. Wooden rackets

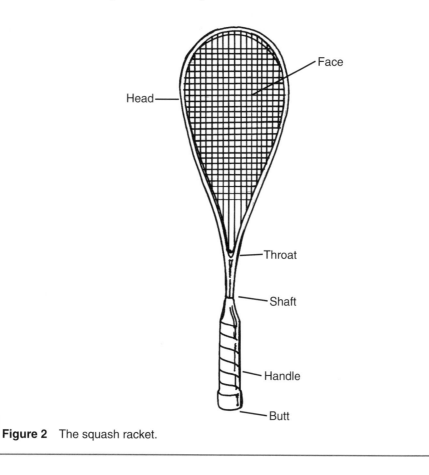

Figure 2 The squash racket.

tended to be quite heavy and flexible; that is, the shaft would bend slightly if the racket head and handle were pulled in the same direction. This flexibility caused a whip as the player swung at the ball, which many players liked at the time because it increased the power of the shot. In the 1980s, however, more players began to use rackets made of graphite. These rackets were lighter, and the racket frames were stiffer. The weight difference added significant extra power to shots, and the stiffness increased control. Graphite rackets gave players such a noticeable advantage that within just a few years wooden rackets became practically obsolete.

The move to graphite rackets was followed by increases in the size of the racket head. Players found that larger racket heads increased the size of the racket's sweet spot—the area of the racket face where the player can gain maximum power with the least vibration. The larger sweet spot was particularly good for beginners, who had more chance of hitting the ball with power.

Today, we are seeing moves toward even lighter, stiffer rackets with larger racket-head sizes, but this kind of racket may not be the best type for you. Try out as many rackets as possible before buying one. You can generally swing lighter rackets faster, creating more power. This is only true, however, if you have a good swing. If you're just learning the game and don't consistently swing well, too light a racket could reduce your power. Rackets now range from about 140 to 240 grams and can be head heavy, evenly balanced, or head light. A racket with a little flexibility can help increase power in your shots, but the trend today is definitely toward the control offered by stiffer frames. Beginners should definitely look for a racket with a large racket head. Often the same racket will be made in several different head sizes, with the size of the head quoted in square centimeters. The largest head size is generally 460 square centimeters. A racket with a head of this size will give the beginner more power and reduce the chances of mis-hitting the ball. The large head size causes a loss in control, and a more experienced player will probably want a midsize head in the range of 380 to 420 square centimeters.

Balls

A squash ball is a hollow rubber ball about two inches in diameter. Squash balls come in a variety of speeds, indicated by a colored dot on the ball. The slowest ball is the yellow dot, used in all tournament play. In ascending order of speed are white, red, and blue dots, with the blue dot being the fastest. A yellow-dot ball is the appropriate one for nearly all games, although beginners may find that a faster ball allows for longer and better rallies. Also, if court conditions are very cold a faster ball may make it easier to have longer rallies.

The most popular squash ball is the Dunlop XX, currently the official ball of the USSRA and used for most tournaments around the world. Prince and Black Knight also make balls used in tournaments.

Squash balls will last only so long. An old ball will often break; the rubber splits and the ball no longer bounces consistently. Even if it isn't broken, you shouldn't use a ball that has become shiny and starts to skid on the floor or off the walls.

Eyewear

In the United States it's mandatory that players wear eyewear when playing squash. Many players feel this is a nuisance because in the middle of a hard game eyewear can feel uncomfortable and the lenses can fog up, leading to restricted vision. The increase in safety, however, easily outweighs the inconvenience. The squash ball is the perfect size to fit into the eye socket. Being hit in the eye with the ball can do serious damage and can even cause blindness.

Choose eyewear that is light but strong enough to withstand a blow from either the ball or the racket. Eyeware ranges in price from $20 to $100. At the top level, Oakley eyeware is the most popular. It is in the higher end of the price range, however, and may not be the best choice for players just beginning the game.

You shouldn't wear eyeware without lenses or with glass lenses. If you wear glasses, you probably won't want to wear your regular glasses, even if they have plastic lenses. The frames are unlikely to be strong enough to protect from a blow from your opponent's racket. You can buy sports glasses that can be fitted with your prescription lenses, or you can buy protective glasses that you can wear over your regular glasses.

If you have a problem with the lenses fogging up, try wearing a headband to reduce the moisture accumulating above your eyes.

Footwear

Squash shoes are similar to shoes worn in other indoor sports such as racquetball, volleyball, and tennis (see figure 3). For regular players a pair of shoes may last only a couple months. Often the toe will wear down before the rest of the shoe because it slides along the floor as you stretch for shots. Shoes with leather toes can reduce this problem, but be wary of the added weight. Make sure that the soles of your shoes are nonmarking. You should never wear running shoes with black soles on the squash court. The soles leave ugly black marks on the floor that are very difficult to remove.

Comfort and durability are major factors in deciding which squash shoes you should buy, but along with this you should consider weight, the grip on the sole, and the support the shoes give. The shoes should be lightweight so you can move quickly, have a strong grip so you feel confident that you won't slide when stretching, and give enough support so you can twist and turn without spraining an ankle.

Toe

Heel

Sole

■ **Figure 3** Squash shoes.

Don't skimp on buying shoes (squash shoes run anywhere from $20 to $100) because you may end up paying for it with a serious injury.

Apparel

Again, squash apparel is similar to that for racquetball and tennis. When squash was played predominantly in private men's clubs, strict rules applied to apparel. Only collared shirts were allowed, and clothes had to be white. Recently, with squash becoming popular with a wider variety of people, many of the old rules have been considerably relaxed. Even in major tournaments colored clothing is normally allowed as long as it is deemed appropriate for squash (beach shorts and tank tops would probably be ruled out!). Some of the major tournaments still require players to wear collared shirts. Otherwise, T-shirts are normally as acceptable as collared shirts.

Apparel is probably the least important item of equipment you buy for squash. As long as you're comfortable, clothing will have little effect on your game, although some people believe that looking good gives them a little more confidence.

STEP 1

THE GRIP AND HANDLING THE RACKET: CONTROLLING THE RACKET FACE

Squash is one of the fastest sports in the world, with the ball often moving at speeds of more than 100 miles per hour. Although the ball loses pace as it rebounds off the front wall, players are often standing only 10 feet or so from the front wall and must react quickly. Professional squash players appear to have almost superhuman reactions. The key is their grip and handling of the racket, which allows them to prepare almost instantaneously for either a forehand or backhand shot.

The grip is difficult to master, especially if you've been playing squash for a while with an incorrect grip. So don't be surprised if you find the correct grip unnatural at first and that your grip moves as you're hitting the ball. Keep working with it, periodically checking to make sure it's correct. In the long run the correct grip will come to feel more comfortable and will greatly improve your shot production.

Don't underestimate the importance of handling the racket properly. One of the biggest problems for beginning players is not having enough time to swing at the ball properly. This lack of time is due to lack of control over the racket face.

Why Is the Grip Important?

The way you grip the racket is important for good stroke production. The correct grip will enable you to keep the racket face open, that is, facing slightly upward. This in turn makes it easier to slice your drop and kill shots, and hit shots out of the back corners. Novice players often grip the racket so that when they swing, the racket face is closed, that is, facing directly at the front wall or downward. This often gives them more power but leads to lack of control and difficulty hitting in the backcourt.

How to Grip the Racket

You should try to use the same grip on both the forehand and the backhand because the speed of the game normally doesn't allow enough time for grip changes. Grip the racket as if you were shaking hands with it (see figure 1.1a). Your thumb and index finger should make a V running down the top inside edge of the racket (that is, the top left edge for right-handed players, the top right edge for left-handed players). Curl your index finger around the racket handle and leave a gap between the index finger and the other three fingers (see figure 1.1b). Gripping the racket with the fingers too close together tends to lead to a lack of control over the racket face. Try to grip the racket handle firmly enough to make sure the racket won't fly out of your hand as you hit the ball but not so tightly that it causes tension in your hand or forearm. It's best to start off by gripping the racket about halfway up the racket handle. Gripping higher on the handle (choking up) helps with control but you lose power, and the reverse is true when you grip lower on the racket handle.

FIGURE
1.1   KEYS TO SUCCESS

THE GRIP

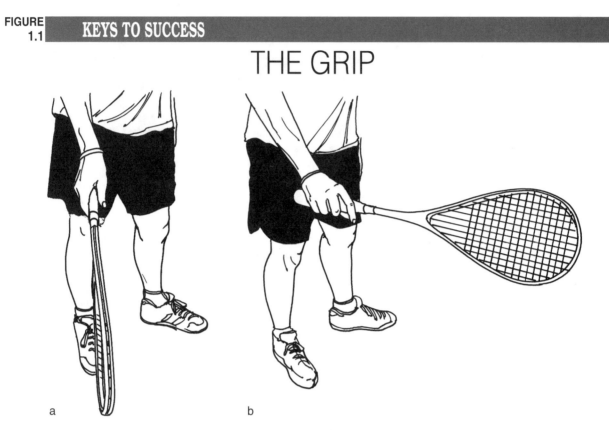

a   b

Execution

1. Grip the racket as if you were shaking hands with it ___
2. Make a V with the thumb and index finger along the inside
   edge of the racket ___
3. Leave a gap between the middle and index finger ___
4. Keep racket face open ___

Why Is Handling the Racket Important?

Improving your racket handling will help you prepare quickly for your shots, giving you more time to concentrate on your swing and on where to hit the ball. Early preparation is the key to timing your strokes well and moving smoothly on the court. By being ready early you'll have many options about where to hit the ball, thus making your shots harder to read.

How to Handle the Racket

Try to keep your wrist cocked so that the racket is at a 90-degree angle to your forearm (see figure 1.2).

The racket face should be open. Hold the racket face steady. You should feel as if you always have total control over the racket face. As you wait for your next shot, concentrate on keeping the racket face from dropping toward your feet. Keep it up at least level with your racket hand. While preparing for your shot make sure your wrist is firm. The racket face should not be moving around too much. Being aware of the exact location of your racket face will help you avoid rushing your shots and will give you the maximum amount of control over your shots.

FIGURE 1.2

KEYS TO SUCCESS

HANDLING THE RACKET

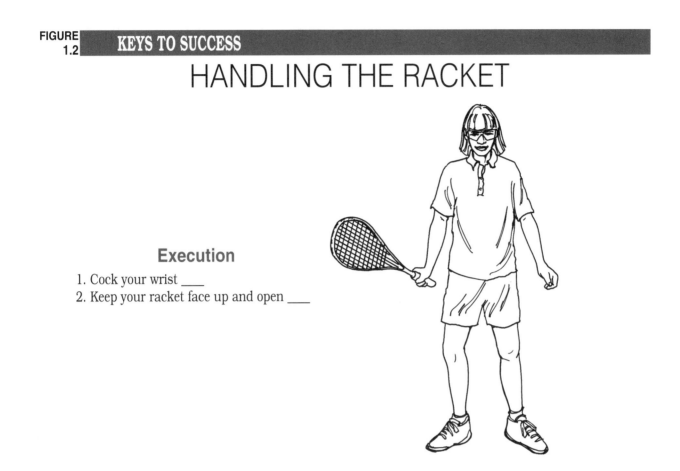

Execution

1. Cock your wrist ___
2. Keep your racket face up and open ___

GRIP AND RACKET HANDLING SUCCESS STOPPERS

It is normally easy to diagnose problems with the grip and racket handling. The problem is making the corrections. The correct way often feels unnatural at first, so you need to check yourself constantly until it becomes habitual to do it the right way.

Error	Correction
1. Shots go down into the tin.	1. Make sure the racket face is open. On the forehand, check that your thumb and index finger are making a V along the top inside edge of the racket. On the backhand, make sure you don't turn your wrist inward.
2. Shots lack control.	2. Make sure you keep your wrist firm throughout the shot.
3. Feeling rushed on shots.	3. Keep your wrist cocked so that the racket face is always up and make sure that you prepare the racket early for your shots.
4. Racket slips while hitting shots.	4. Grip the racket a little tighter.
5. Hand becomes tired from hitting shots.	5. Don't grip the racket quite so tightly.

GRIP AND RACKET HANDLING

DRILLS

1. Roll Ball Around Racket Face

Make sure you grip the racket in the correct manner. Hold the racket out in front of you. Turn your wrist so that your knuckles are facing down and the racket face is parallel to the floor. Place the ball on the racket strings and roll it around the racket face for as long as you can before it falls off. Then twist your wrist so that your knuckles and the other side of the racket face are facing up and repeat the exercise.

Success Goal =

60 seconds without the ball falling from the racket face (knuckles down) ___

60 seconds without the ball falling from the racket face (knuckles up) ___

✔ Success Check

• Keep racket face parallel to the floor ___
• Move the ball at a controlled pace ___

To Increase Difficulty

• Do the exercise with your eyes closed.
• Walk around the court while doing the exercise.

To Decrease Difficulty

• Choke up on the racket.
• Keep the ball moving at a slower pace or not at all.

2. Bounce Ball on Racket Face

Hold the racket as you did in the first drill but this time bounce the ball on the racket face as many times as you can. As you do, try to maintain the proper grip.

Success Goal = 20 bounces in a row ___

Success Check
- Keep a firm grip ___
- Use a short, controlled, punchy movement with the racket face ___

To Increase Difficulty
- Bounce the ball higher in the air.
- Walk around the court while bouncing ball on racket face.

To Decrease Difficulty
- Choke up on the racket.
- Use any grip necessary to keep drill going.

3. Racket Blocks

Stand about 15 feet from a partner with your racket face up, holding your racket in front of your body. Have your partner throw balls alternately to each side of your body. Stop the ball with your racket face, letting the ball fall to the floor and roll back to your partner.

Success Goal = 8 out of 10 successful blocks ___

Success Check
- Hold the racket firmly ___
- Keep your wrist cocked ___
- Watch the ball onto the racket face ___

To Increase Difficulty
- Have partner throw randomly to either side of your body.
- Have two partners throw to you to increase the speed of the drill.

To Decrease Difficulty
- Have partner throw the ball more slowly.
- Have partner throw only to one side.

4. Racket Catches

Stand about six feet from a wall. Throw the ball against the wall and then catch it on your racket face. Try to cradle the ball with your racket face as you do when you catch a ball with your hands and pull it into your chest. By moving the racket face down as you catch the ball, you'll prevent it from bouncing off the strings.

Success Goal = 5 out of 10 successful catches ___

Success Check
- Cradle the ball with the racket face ___
- Watch the ball onto the racket face ___

To Increase Difficulty
- Have a partner hit the ball onto the wall for you to catch on your racket face.

To Decrease Difficulty
- Throw the ball in the air and catch it on your racket face.

GRIP AND RACKET HANDLING SUCCESS SUMMARY

Achieving the correct grip on the racket is difficult, but it's the key to good shot production. Always pretend you're shaking hands with the racket so that you form a V with the inside edge of the racket. Remember not to grip so tightly that you strain your wrist or forearm but keep your wrist firm throughout the shot. Always keep the wrist cocked and the racket face open. After you've completed the drills, ask a partner to check your fundamentals using the Keys to Success checklists in figures 1.1 and 1.2.

STEP 2

BASIC FOREHAND AND BACKHAND SWINGS:
DEVELOPING SOLID FUNDAMENTALS

All top-level squash players have one thing in common: the ability to hit consistent drives accurately into the back corners of the court. This consistency comes from having solid fundamentals on their basic forehand and backhand swings. The object of this step is to introduce you to the keys to the basic forehand and backhand swings so that you can hit your drives with power and pinpoint accuracy.

A drive is a shot hit after the ball has bounced on the floor. A forehand drive is hit on the side of your body where you hold the racket. A backhand drive is hit on the opposite side of your body. You'll need to be prepared to hit forehand and backhand drives from all areas of the court.

Most beginners find the forehand swing easier at first because its motion is similar to the one you use when you hit a baseball or swing a golf club. The motion, in fact, is almost identical to that of throwing a stone when you're trying to skim it across water. As you begin to practice the correct swings, however, you'll probably find that the motion on the backhand side is more natural.

Why Is the Forehand Swing Important?

Many people find that they can pick up a squash racket for the first time and hit the ball quite hard on the forehand side. But building the necessary accuracy into the forehand shots is often difficult. For this reason it's important to learn the basic elements of the swing. These elements will apply to all your forehand shots, regardless of whether you're in the backcourt, in the frontcourt, attacking, or defending.

How to Perform the Forehand Swing

When you are hitting the ball on the forehand, keep in mind that the power is coming from the backswing, not from the follow-through. To achieve this you must try to position yourself so that your front shoulder is turned toward the side wall and your back is almost facing the front wall (see figure 2.1a). Your front foot should be closer to the side wall than your back foot. You should hold your racket high, with your elbow away from your body and bent at no more than a 90-degree angle. Cock your wrist so that you hold the racket face almost directly above your head.

The swing is a U-shaped swing: Bring the racket face down, through the ball, and then up on the follow-through in one continuous motion (see figure 2.1b). You should be trying to make contact with the ball to the side of your front foot. Keep your arm straight and your wrist cocked so that the racket face is at the same level as your hand. Keep the racket face open on contact so that you can hit up through the ball. It's important to keep your wrist firm throughout the shot so that you push through the ball rather than snap your wrist. Your hips will start off facing the back corner and will turn slightly toward the side wall on the backswing, but as you make contact with the ball and follow through, they should stay still and be facing the side wall at the end of the swing. You should be getting the power in the shot from your shoulders, not from your wrist or hips.

Make sure that you prepare your racket early but try to avoid stepping across with your front foot too soon. The step should come just before you begin the swing, and you should bend your leading leg so that you transfer your weight to the front foot as you begin the backswing. You should bring the racket face through the ball quickly to generate power in the shot, but don't try to hit the ball too hard. Keep the swing relaxed and put your effort into bending down to the ball rather than trying to muscle it with your body.

Keep your eyes fixed on the ball throughout the shot and try to hit the ball at a comfortable distance from your body. Don't hit the ball at the top of the bounce; by letting it start to drop you'll find it much easier to hit the ball up and send it into the back corners.

As you swing through, drop your front shoulder and position your body in a crouched position so that your head is over the ball (see figure 2.1c). Make sure you keep your head still throughout the swing and stay as balanced as possible.

FIGURE 2.1

KEYS TO SUCCESS

FOREHAND SWING

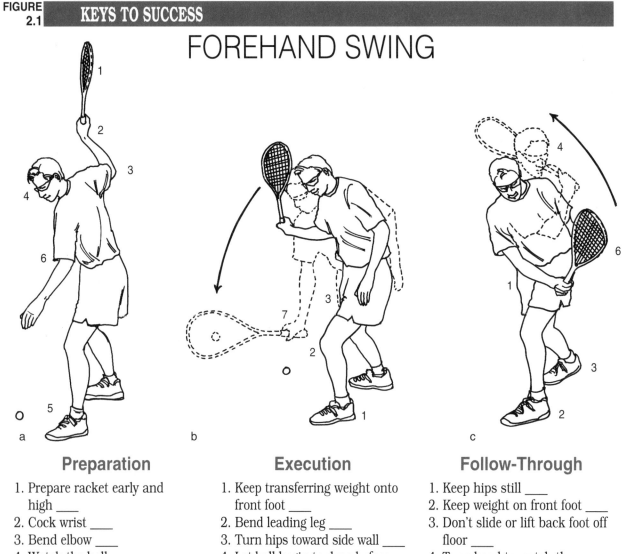

Preparation

1. Prepare racket early and high ___
2. Cock wrist ___
3. Bend elbow ___
4. Watch the ball ___
5. Step across on front foot ___
6. Drop front shoulder and point it toward side wall ___

Execution

1. Keep transferring weight onto front foot ___
2. Bend leading leg ___
3. Turn hips toward side wall ___
4. Let ball begin to drop before making contact ___
5. Contact ball to the side of the front foot ___
6. Keep racket face open ___
7. Keep wrist firm and cocked ___

Follow-Through

1. Keep hips still ___
2. Keep weight on front foot ___
3. Don't slide or lift back foot off floor ___
4. Turn head to watch the ball ___
5. Bend elbow ___
6. Bring racket face up to front shoulder ___

Why Is the Backhand Swing Important?

Unlike the forehand, the backhand is at first often very difficult for the beginner. If the player can make contact at all, it can seem nearly impossible to hit a backhand shot with any power. Players who don't learn the basic principles of the backhand swing will constantly find it the weak part of their game. Their opponents will be looking to seize any chance to hit the ball to the backhand side of the court, forcing many errors and poor returns.

If you learn and practice the basic components, however, you'll find the backhand swing is a natural motion. These rudiments will improve all your backhand shots.

How to Perform the Backhand Swing

As with the forehand, the power on the backhand should come from the backswing, not the follow-through. So again you must try to position yourself so that your front shoulder is turned toward the side wall and your back is almost facing the front wall (see figure 2.2a). Having your front foot closer to the side wall than your back foot will facilitate your body positioning. Your racket face should be behind the back of your neck, and your racket hand must be close to your back shoulder. Keep your wrist cocked and firm so that your racket face is steady before you swing. Your elbow should be in close to your body and should be pointing downward, not toward the side wall. This will make it much easier to get your shoulders into the shot.

As you swing, the racket face will again follow a U shape, coming down on the backswing, through the ball, and then up on the follow-through (see figure 2.2b). Try to make contact with the ball to the side of your body a few inches forward from your front foot. Keep your arm straight and your wrist cocked so that

the racket face doesn't drop below the level of your hand. Make sure again that your racket face is open as you make contact with the ball and that you keep your wrist firm, pushing through the ball instead of snapping the wrist. Your hips will turn from facing the back corner at the start of the backswing to facing the side wall as you strike the ball. Again, keep your hips still as you make contact and follow through.

The timing of your shoulder turn, your step into the shot, and your swing are crucial to hitting with power and control on the backhand. Try to think about it in three stages. First, prepare your racket early (when you see it's going to be a backhand) and begin to turn your body so that you face the side wall. Then, as the ball approaches, slowly begin to turn, drop your front shoulder, and pull your elbow back around your body so that you are getting a good windup for the shot. Finally, after the ball has bounced, step across with your front foot and swing through. Make sure that the swing comes immediately after the step, that you bend your leading leg, and that you keep your weight on the front foot throughout the shot.

The racket face needs to come through the ball quickly to generate power in the shot, but again, don't try to muscle the shot with your body. Relax as you swing and put your effort into bending down. Don't let your back foot slide or lift off the ground as you strike the ball. Also try to keep your head still. Again, watch the ball constantly and try to hit the ball at a comfortable distance from your body. As with the forehand, let the ball begin to drop from the top of its bounce before you strike it so that it will be easier to hit up through the shot.

Bend your elbow on the follow-through and bring the racket face up so that it finishes almost above your head (see figure 2.2c). Keeping your body still and controlling your racket face on the follow-through will not only improve the accuracy of your shots but also keep you from having an excessive, dangerous swing that could injure your opponent.

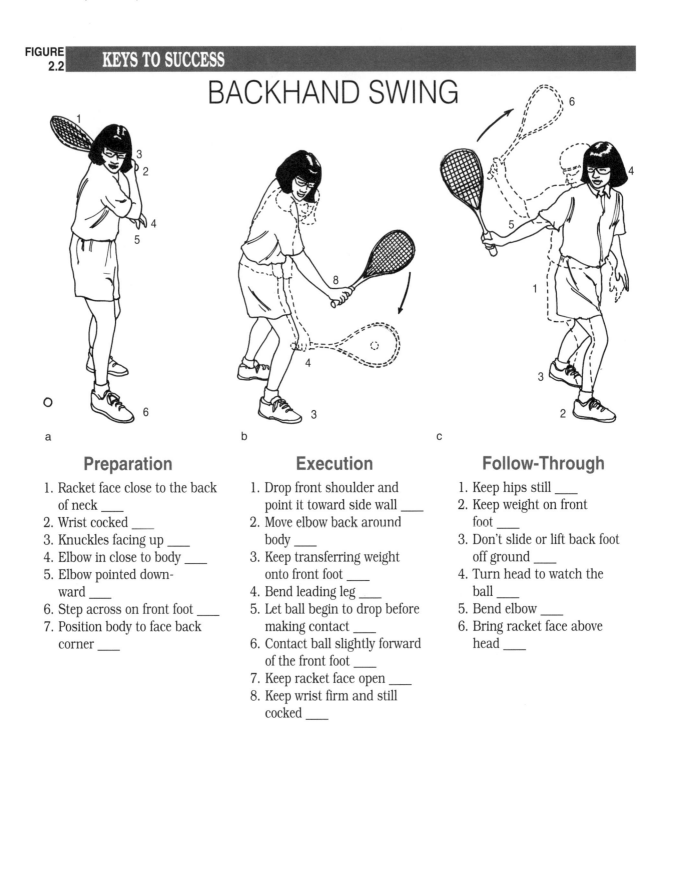

FIGURE
2.2 **KEYS TO SUCCESS**

BACKHAND SWING

a

b

c

Preparation

1. Racket face close to the back of neck ___
2. Wrist cocked ___
3. Knuckles facing up ___
4. Elbow in close to body ___
5. Elbow pointed downward ___
6. Step across on front foot ___
7. Position body to face back corner ___

Execution

1. Drop front shoulder and point it toward side wall ___
2. Move elbow back around body ___
3. Keep transferring weight onto front foot ___
4. Bend leading leg ___
5. Let ball begin to drop before making contact ___
6. Contact ball slightly forward of the front foot ___
7. Keep racket face open ___
8. Keep wrist firm and still cocked ___

Follow-Through

1. Keep hips still ___
2. Keep weight on front foot ___
3. Don't slide or lift back foot off ground ___
4. Turn head to watch the ball ___
5. Bend elbow ___
6. Bring racket face above head ___

BASIC FOREHAND AND BACKHAND SWING SUCCESS STOPPERS

It's often difficult to recognize exactly what you're doing wrong when you have problems with your basic swing. Here are the most common errors and the ways you can adjust your swing to correct them.

Error	Correction
1. Shot lacks enough power to reach the back wall before bouncing twice.	1. Make sure you start with the racket up high on the backswing and your shoulder turned so that your back is almost facing the front wall. Bring racket face through the ball more quickly but try to keep your body still. Make sure that you time the step into the shot with your front foot just before you begin the swing.
2. Ball goes down the middle of the court.	2. You hit the ball too far forward; wait longer and try to hit it to the side of your front foot.
3. Ball goes into the side wall.	3. Either the ball got too far behind you or, more likely, you moved your hips toward the front wall as you made contact and followed through.
4. Ball went too low on the front wall.	4. Bend your knees more, make sure you keep your racket face open, and keep your wrist firm throughout the swing.
5. Completely missed the ball or didn't make solid contact.	5. Keep your eyes on the ball as you swing, take your time, and stay still as you make contact.

BASIC FOREHAND AND BACKHAND SWING

DRILLS

1. Shadow Swings

Practice forehand and backhand swings in front of a mirror. Check to make sure that you're using a high backswing and try to avoid snapping your wrist as you follow through. If you don't have a large mirror you can try watching yourself in the glass back wall of a squash court.

Success Goal = 50 alternating forehand and backhand swings ____

Success Check
• Use a U-shaped swing ____
• Transfer weight onto your front foot as you swing ____

To Increase Difficulty
• Close your eyes and visualize your swing.

To Decrease Difficulty
• Break down the swing into stages and practice each stage separately—backswing, contact, and follow-through.

2. Hit Shots Past the Short Line

Position yourself about halfway between the front wall and the short line and about five feet from the side wall. Stand with your racket prepared and your body facing the side wall. Throw the ball against the side wall so that it bounces about four feet away from you and directly between you and the side wall. When it bounces on the floor, step across with your front foot, turn your front shoulder toward the side wall, and then swing through. Try to hit the ball straight so that it stays close to the side wall and deep enough so that it bounces past the short line. Do this drill on both the forehand and backhand sides. If you have problems getting the ball deep enough, bend your knees more and try to aim your shot higher on the front wall.

Success Goal =

8 out of 10 forehand shots bouncing past the short line ___

8 out of 10 backhand shots bouncing past the short line ___

Success Check

• Prepare your racket before throwing the ball ___
• Throw the ball so that it bounces in line with your front foot ___
• Aim high on the front wall ___

To Increase Difficulty

• Hit the ball deeper in the court.
• Hit the ball above the cut line.
• Hit crosscourt toward the opposite back corner.

To Decrease Difficulty

• Concentrate only on making contact; don't worry about where the ball goes.

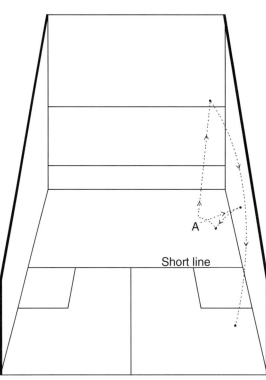

Short line

3. Target Drives

This is the same as drill 2, except you should stand on the short line and try to hit the ball so that it bounces on a target placed against the side wall about two feet behind the back of the service box.

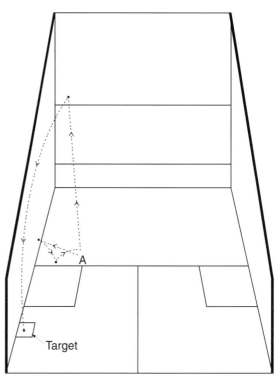

Success Goal = 5 out of 10 shots hitting the target ___

Success Check
- Time your step and swing to increase power ___
- Swing through fast while keeping your body still ___
- Avoid snapping your wrist ___

To Increase Difficulty
- Vary the pace of your shots.
- Hit crosscourt at a target in the opposite back corner.

To Decrease Difficulty
- Make the target area larger.
- Concentrate solely on making good contact with the ball.

Target

A

4. Hit From Partner's Drop

Stand on the T (the intersection of the short line and the half-court line) and have a partner stand to the side of you about six feet away. The partner should drop the ball about two feet away from you. Let the ball bounce, reach the top of its bounce, and start to drop. Then swing and hit a straight drive toward the back corner.

Success Goal = 8 out of 10 shots bouncing behind the short line ____

Success Check
- Watch the ball ____
- Bend your knees ____
- Keep your head still as you swing ____

To Increase Difficulty
- Aim higher on the front wall.
- Alternate straight and crosscourt drives.
- Set a target to aim at.

To Decrease Difficulty
- Shorten your backswing and concentrate only on striking the ball.

5. Hit Shots From Partner's Feed

Have a partner stand in the back corner and hit short shots to the front of the court. From the T, step across toward the ball and hit straight drives off the feeds to the back corner, keeping the ball close to the side wall. Try to keep the shots no farther from the side wall than the width of the service box. If possible your partner should keep the drill going without stopping between shots.

Success Goal = 10 consecutive shots bouncing past the back of the service box ____

Success Check
- Watch the ball as your partner strikes it ____
- Don't get too close to the ball ____
- Push through as you make contact ____

To Increase Difficulty
- Have your partner feed lower shots, forcing you to bend more.
- Set a target in the back corner to aim at.

To Decrease Difficulty
- Have your partner feed higher shots.
- Have your partner stop after each shot so you have time to prepare for the next one.

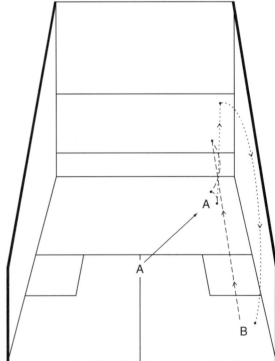

6. Crosscourt Rallies

Stand near the back service box on one side of the court. Have a partner stand near the back of the service box on the opposite side. Throw the ball against the side wall closer to you. After it has bounced on the floor hit the ball against the front wall so that it rebounds toward your partner. Your partner then hits the ball back to you. Try to keep a rally going as long as you can. To hit the ball so that it travels across the court to your partner, make contact slightly farther forward from your front foot and aim for the middle of the front wall. Make sure that you hit forehands on the forehand side and backhands on the backhand side (that is, move toward the middle of the court so that you can hit the ball between your body and the side wall closer to you).

 **Success Goal** = 20 consecutive shots between you and your partner ___

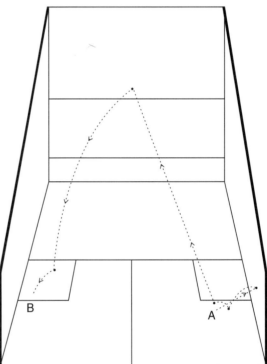

Success Check
- Hit slightly forward from your front foot ___
- Prepare your racket early ___
- Aim at center of the front wall ___

To Increase Difficulty
- Stand farther back in the court.
- Keep increasing the number of consecutive shots by 10 until you reach 50.

BASIC FOREHAND AND BACKHAND SWING SUCCESS SUMMARY

Developing a solid basic swing is fundamental because all other swings are based upon it. Remember to prepare your racket early, keep your wrist cocked, bend your knees, and keep your trunk and feet still as you swing through the shot. Swing through quickly but always concentrate on allowing your shoulders, not your hips, to give power to your shot. And, of course, always keep your eye on the ball.

Once you've completed the drills for both the forehand and backhand swings, ask a partner to check your fundamentals using the Keys to Success checklists for the basic swing in figures 2.1 and 2.2.

STEP 3

COURT MOVEMENT: IMPROVING FOOTWORK AND STAMINA

Some top players move so gracefully around the court that they make the game look effortless. You'll soon find out, if you haven't already, that squash is a game that is rarely effortless. What is the secret to this seeming contradiction? Certainly the hours of hard physical training that top players put in is one reason. But that isn't all; their knowledge of correct court movement is just as important.

Now that you have an understanding of the basic swing, it's time to look at the way you move around the court. Good court movement will bring your basic game together. You'll be able to position yourself better for your shots. You'll be able to cover your opponent's shots quickly and thus have more time to play your own.

Why Is Court Movement Important?

Good court movement is important for two main reasons. First, it will allow you to cover the court more quickly and more efficiently. Second, it will help you to position yourself better for your shots. Players who haven't developed good movement constantly find themselves out of position, rushing madly around the court trying to keep the ball in play. It's often such an effort to get to the ball that it's difficult to think about anything else, such as stroke production and strategy. These players improve only slowly, if at all, because in game situations they're never in control of their shots and thus can never work on improving their strokes.

If you work on your court movement you'll soon find that your balance and composure on court will improve. Smooth movement will eventually become

second nature, and you'll then be able to concentrate on your strokes and on developing good basic strategy.

How to Move on the Court

It is important to keep your movement as smooth and as unhurried as possible. Balance is key. Keep on the balls of your feet, ready to move in any direction to retrieve your opponent's shot. If you're in reasonable position watching your opponent strike the ball, you'll nearly always have plenty of time to retrieve the shot. So don't rush. Take your time and concentrate on moving to a sideways position a reasonable distance from the ball.

Good movement consists of a combination of quick short steps, shuffle steps, and long strides to the ball. Your movement will be similar to that of a boxer: Stay balanced with little shuffles before taking a big step when going for the punch. Use little steps around the T so that you are nicely balanced to move in any direction to the ball, and then use larger steps as your final steps to the ball to cover the court efficiently.

Frontcourt Movement

As you move in the frontcourt from the T to the ball, begin by taking small steps so that you keep balanced. Then take a couple of large steps into the shot. Move in a slight J shape, rather than straight at the ball, to help you get into a sideways position to play the shot (see figure 3.1). Try to time your movement forward so that your second-to-last step is with your back foot. You then pivot on this foot, turning your front shoulder toward the side wall and preparing the racket. Your final step with your front foot should come just before your swing.

As you strike the ball, keep your back foot still so that you can push off your front foot after you have finished the follow-through. This will enable you to move quickly back to the middle of the court. Keep facing the front wall (but turn your head to watch the ball) as you backpedal directly back to the T. Make sure, however, that your movement back to the T doesn't impede your opponent from moving directly to the ball.

KEYS TO SUCCESS

FRONTCOURT MOVEMENT

Execution

1. Move in a J shape ____
2. Pivot on the back foot ____
3. Step across on front foot ____
4. Push off front foot ____
5. Backpedal to the T ____

Midcourt Movement

A common mistake players make when moving in the midcourt is turning toward the side wall while they are on the T and then running straight at the ball. This is not only an inefficient way of moving, it also makes it difficult to change direction if the ball does not go where you expect. Instead when you move sideways from the T in the midcourt, move with a shuffling or side-stepping motion (see figure 3.2). This will allow you to stay balanced and will make it easier for you to make final adjustments to get into good hitting position. When moving to the side, one side step is normally enough. Pivot on your back foot again to get the front foot across. Your back foot should stay as still as possible as you strike the ball, enabling you to push back to the middle of the court off the front foot. Then, just step directly back to the T, ready to move for your next shot.

FIGURE
3.2

KEYS TO SUCCESS

MIDCOURT MOVEMENT

Execution

1. Side step across the court ___
2. Pivot on back foot ___
3. Step across on front foot ___
4. Step back to the T ___

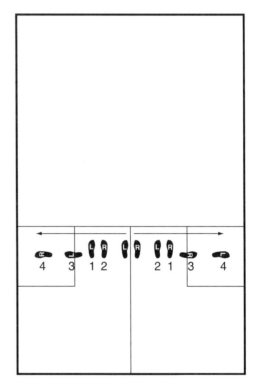

Backcourt Movement

The movement to the back of the court is the most difficult. It is easy to end up too close to the ball to make a good swing. Again, use the J-shaped movement and the shuffling or side-stepping motion. Move back and then across to the ball (see figure 3.3). Ideally, you'll want to get into the midstance, that is, with your feet about shoulder-width apart and almost parallel to the side wall. Often it works best to position your feet quickly and then make some final small shuffles to adjust to the correct position for hitting the ball. Sometimes, however, you won't have time to get into the midstance; it will be necessary to pivot on the back foot and step across to the ball on the front foot as you did at the front and the side. After hitting out of the back corner, step toward the half-court line with your front foot if you hit a straight drive (to give your opponent a direct line to the ball); otherwise, you can move straight to the T.

During a rally you may find that you're unable to recover to the T before your opponent hits a shot and that you have more of the court to cover. In this case, take large steps to cover the court quickly and stretch with your last step so that you can reach out farther with the racket face and get lower down to the ball. Stretching and bending are the keys to the amazing retrievals made by top players. Remember that when you're out of position, desperate measures are often required to get the ball back into play. It may be necessary to step across on the wrong foot or make the wrong movement to get the ball back. Side stepping to the back corner, for example, isn't practical if you have to cover much of the court in a short time.

FIGURE 3.3

KEYS TO SUCCESS

BACKCOURT MOVEMENT

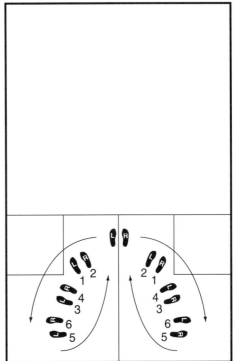

Execution

1. Side step when possible (see numbers 1 through 6) ___
2. Move back and then across ___
3. Use the midstance ___
4. Step back toward the half-court line ___

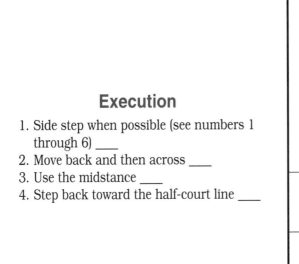

Developing good court movement, however, is only half the battle. When you come up against an opponent who hits and moves as well as you do, there will be no substitute for having the fitness to outlast your opponent. Squash demands a mixture of endurance and speed, so any off-court training you do to help your fitness should include both attributes. Don't do too much long-distance running because this will make you slow on court; instead, vary your training to include some sessions of short sprints and some two- to four-mile runs. Nothing is better for your squash fitness, though, than simulating movements made on the court. The "ghosting" drills described later in this step will not only help you improve your court movement but also serve as a fitness routine.

COURT MOVEMENT SUCCESS STOPPERS

The ghosting drills in this step will help you iron out most problems with your court movement. The following is a list of the most common problems with court movement and corrections you can make to solve them.

Error	Correction
1. You're consistently too close to the ball.	1. Don't rush at the ball; take your time and concentrate on moving smoothly.
2. You are badly positioned to hit the ball.	2. Make sure you use the J-shaped movement rather than running straight at the ball.
3. Too slow off the mark to the ball.	3. Keep balanced and on the balls of your feet and make sure you constantly watch the ball.
4. You constantly have too much court to cover to retrieve the ball.	4. Make sure that you move back to the T after your shot.

COURT MOVEMENT

DRILLS

The best drills for court movement are ghosting exercises, in which you move from the T to the corners or sides of the court, play an imaginary (shadow) stroke, and then move back to the T again. When ghosting, you must use the correct footwork and play a proper stroke. Avoid just sticking the racket out. Prepare and swing as if you were going to hit the ball. You should try to do ghosting quickly without compromising the quality of your movement and swing.

1. Front Corners

Start on the T. Run forward, in a J shape, to one of the front corners, play an imaginary straight drive, and then backpedal to the T. Make sure that you move back behind the short line before you move forward and repeat in the other front corner. Use figure 3.1 as a guide to your footwork. Time yourself to see how long it takes you to do 30 ghosts (15 in each corner).

Success Goal = 30 ghosts in under 2 1/2 minutes ____

Success Check
• Use J-shaped movement ____
• Prepare racket early ____
• Backpedal to T ____

To Decrease Difficulty
• Don't time yourself; concentrate instead on the quality of your movement.

2. Side to Side

Start on the T. Side step across, turn, and play an imaginary shot with your forehand. Push back off your front foot toward the T, making sure you turn toward the front wall, not away from it. Then side step across the court, turn, and hit an imaginary backhand shot. Use figure 3.2 as a guide to your footwork. Time yourself to see how long it takes you to do 50 ghosts (25 on each side).

 **Success Goal** = 50 ghosts in under 2 minutes ___

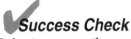 **Success Check**
- Side step across the court ___
- Pivot on your back foot ___
- Step across on your front foot ___

To Increase Difficulty
- Use only one side step across the court; then turn and stretch across with your front foot as far as possible.

To Decrease Difficulty
- Don't time yourself; concentrate instead on the quality of your movement.

3. Back Corners

Start on the T. Turn and side step toward a back corner; then take a small step across with your front foot and play an imaginary straight drive. Push off your front foot and then side step back through the T toward the other back corner. Use figure 3.3 as a guide to your footwork. Time yourself to see how long it takes to do 30 ghosts (15 on each side).

 **Success Goal** = 30 ghosts in under 2 minutes ___

To Decrease Difficulty
- Don't time yourself; concentrate instead on the quality of your movement.

Success Check
- Use side-stepping movement ___
- Prepare racket early ___
- Move to and from the T ___

4. Star Drills

This drill combines the first three drills. Move from the T to the front corners and play imaginary shots, then to the sides, and then to the back corners. Try to make your movements through the T as smooth as possible; don't stop at the T but move in one continuous motion from one shot to the next. Playing imaginary shots at each of the six points is one star; try to complete five stars in as short a time as possible.

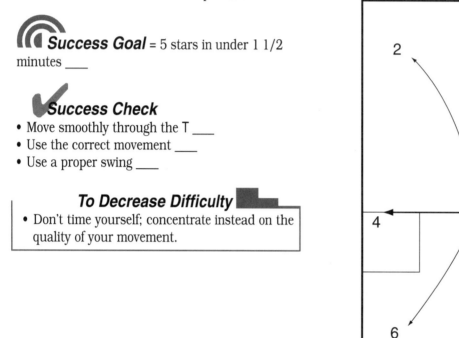

Success Goal = 5 stars in under 1 1/2 minutes ___

Success Check
• Move smoothly through the T ___
• Use the correct movement ___
• Use a proper swing ___

To Decrease Difficulty
• Don't time yourself; concentrate instead on the quality of your movement.

5. Random Ghosts

Number from 1 to 6 the four corners and the two sides. Have a partner stand against the front wall and randomly call out numbers from 1 through 6. You must move from the T to the corresponding area, play an imaginary shot, and return to the T. Your partner should call out the next number just as you are returning to the T so that you must move to the next position with little hesitation. It can be difficult to remember the corresponding areas while doing this drill, but this is beneficial because you must move while thinking about something else. Therefore, your partner should make you think for yourself by refraining from pointing to the area to which you should be moving.

Success Goal = 30 imaginary shots in under 2 minutes ___

Success Check
• Step across on your front foot ___
• Move through the T ___
• Use a proper swing ___

To Decrease Difficulty
• Don't time yourself; concentrate instead on the quality of your movement.

COURT MOVEMENT SUCCESS SUMMARY

You might be fit and have good strokes, but if you don't move efficiently around the court your opponent can easily and repeatedly catch you off guard. Good court movement consists of allowing yourself enough room to hit the ball, moving smoothly to and from the center of the court, and remaining balanced and ready by staying on the balls of your feet and by using the correct stance for a given shot. The ghosting drills in this step will be helpful for both your court movement and fitness but only if you concentrate on using proper footwork and stroke production. Have a partner monitor your court movement skills using the Keys to Success checklists in figures 3.1 through 3.3.

STEP 4

MOVING AND HITTING WITHIN THE FRONTCOURT: DEVELOPING PATIENCE TO HIT THE BALL

op-level players move and hit so well at the front of the court that they can gain a decisive advantage from the slightest inaccurate shot to the front court from their opponents. They can pounce quickly onto any shot that is not hit just above the tin or close to the side wall and dispatch the ball deep into the back corners. This forces their opponents to scramble quickly back to stay in the rally.

Now that you've learned the basic swing and correct court movement, it's time to start putting the two together. When moving and hitting at the front of the court, you should be patient and move smoothly. Most beginners rush around the court and often find themselves too close to the ball and off balance when trying to make their shots. One reason that players rush so much is that they don't realize how much time they have.

Why Is Moving and Hitting Within the Frontcourt Important?

Because they haven't yet developed an understanding of good basic strategy, low-level players play the majority of their shots low on the front wall into the frontcourt area. If you can't move and hit well from the front of the court, you'll find yourself giving up easy points against these low-level players. Learning some basic ideas about moving and hitting in the frontcourt will enable you to elevate your game. You'll force your opponents to hit lower on the front wall, which will cause them to make more errors. To pressure you, they'll have to hit shots deeper in the court.

How to Move Within the Frontcourt

After every shot you should try to move to the middle of the court (the T), because from there you'll be able to cover all four corners. If, after hitting, you wait for your opponent to hit before moving, you'll occasionally be lucky and have the ball returned to you. But more often than not you'll find yourself working twice as hard as you should, chasing the ball across the court.

Try to get to the T before your opponent hits the ball, but don't move so fast that you can't concentrate on watching the ball and staying balanced, ready to change direction quickly. Balance is everything; with it you're able to retrieve many more of your opponent's shots because you're always ready to move quickly in any direction.

When you are on the T waiting for your opponent to hit, keep on the balls of your feet with your racket slightly to your side and the racket face up. Letting the racket face fall to your feet will cause you to take more time preparing for your shot, which often leads to rushed strokes. Don't stand with your body facing straight at the front wall. Instead turn your body 45 degrees so that it's facing the front corner of the side from which your opponent is hitting (see figure 4.1). From this position you'll be able to turn easily and watch the ball, even if it's right in the back corner. Always watch the ball, especially while your opponent is hitting it. It's easy to turn away from the ball a fraction of a second too soon and end up moving the wrong way.

Figure 4.1 Be in a ready position at the T in preparation to return your opponent's shot.

When moving to the ball in the front corners, think about moving to a position to the side of the ball. Don't run straight at the ball because you'll end up too close to the ball to make a smooth swing. Instead move in a slight J shape and begin to turn your front shoulder. Pivot on your back foot before making your last step with your front foot into the shot (see figure 4.2). This will help you get into a sideways position to strike the

Figure 4.2 Move to a position beside the ball before striking it.

ball. Try not to rush; remember that good timing will increase your power and control. Keep your movement and swing as effortless as possible.

How to Hit Within the Frontcourt

Remember to prepare the racket early, well before you make the last step into the shot (see figures 4.3a and 4.4a). You should time your movement to the ball so that your final step is with your front foot just before you begin your swing. Your movement and preparation should be the same regardless of whether you are hitting the ball straight or crosscourt. The only difference is that you should strike a straight shot level with your front foot (see figures 4.3b and 4.4b) and a crosscourt shot slightly farther forward (see figures 4.5 and 4.6). While striking the ball, keep your back foot still; don't let it slide or lift completely off the floor. This will help you keep your body still and maintain control of the shot. After you've followed through with the shot, push back off your front foot and backpedal toward the T (see figures 4.3c and 4.4c).

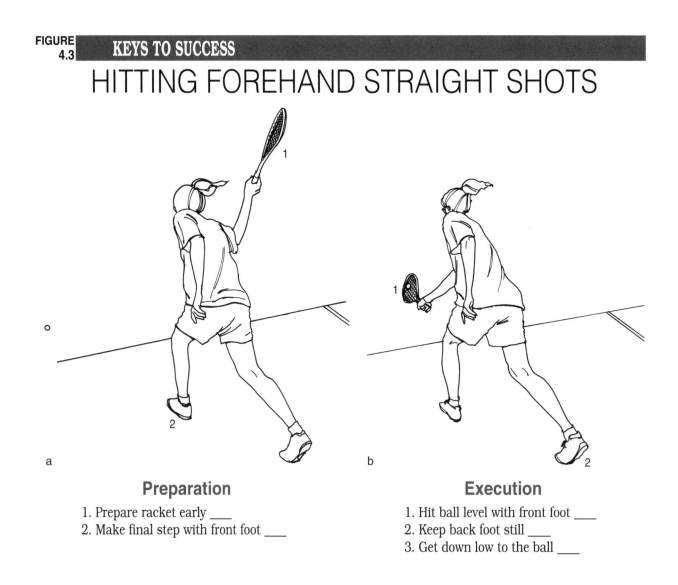

**FIGURE
4.3**   **KEYS TO SUCCESS**

HITTING FOREHAND STRAIGHT SHOTS

a

b

Preparation
1. Prepare racket early ___
2. Make final step with front foot ___

Execution
1. Hit ball level with front foot ___
2. Keep back foot still ___
3. Get down low to the ball ___

Follow-Through

1. Bring racket up ___
2. Push back off front foot ___
3. Backpedal to T ___

FIGURE 4.4

KEYS TO SUCCESS

HITTING BACKHAND STRAIGHT SHOTS

a

b

c

Preparation

1. Prepare racket early ___
2. Make final step with front foot ___

Execution

1. Hit ball level with front foot ___
2. Keep back foot still ___
3. Get down low to the ball ___

Follow-Through

1. Bring racket up ___
2. Push back off front foot ___
3. Backpedal to T ___

FIGURE 4.5

KEYS TO SUCCESS

HITTING FOREHAND CROSSCOURT SHOTS

Execution

1. Hit ball just forward from your front foot ___
2. Make sure shot has plenty of width ___
3. Recover to T quickly and smoothly ___

FIGURE 4.6 **KEYS TO SUCCESS**

HITTING BACKHAND CROSSCOURT SHOTS

Execution

1. Hit ball just forward from your front foot ___
2. Make sure shot has plenty of width ___
3. Recover to T quickly and smoothly ___

You should begin by hitting drives into the back corners (later steps cover shots to the front of the court). Hit your drives with good depth and good width—deep enough to take your opponent into the back corners and wide enough that your opponent can't cut them off. Try to keep your straight drives close to the side wall, with the first bounce just beyond the service box so that the second bounce is close to the back wall (see figure 4.7). Your crosscourt drives should have enough width to hit the side wall toward the back of the service box. The ball should then bounce on the floor close to the back wall (see figure 4.8). Don't aim your crosscourts straight at the back corner. The ball will pass through the middle of the court where your opponent can cut it off before it reaches the back of the court.

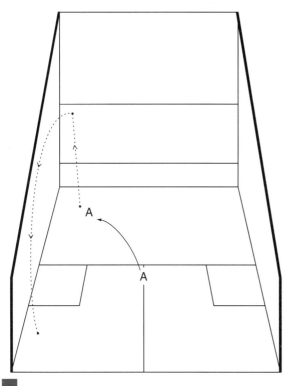

Figure 4.7 Player movement and path of ball for a straight drive.

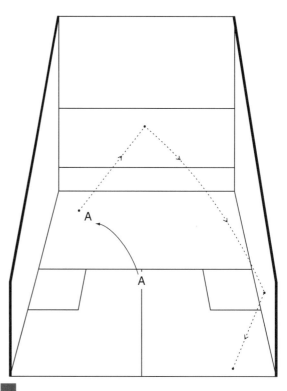

Figure 4.8 Player movement and path of ball for a crosscourt drive.

MOVING AND HITTING WITHIN THE FRONTCOURT SUCCESS STOPPERS

When you've hit a shot to the backcourt, you should feel confident about covering any shot your opponent hits to the front. If you don't yet have this confidence you must continue to work hard on your moving and hitting within the frontcourt. The following is a list of the most common errors with this aspect of the game and suggestions to correct them.

Error	Correction
1. Too late reacting to opponent's shot; unable to hit ball.	1. Make sure you keep your eye on the ball. Don't turn away from your opponent until he or she has hit a shot.

Error	Correction
2. Feeling rushed when striking the ball.	2. Prepare your racket when you see to which side the ball is going. This will give you more time to position yourself and strike the ball.
3. Too close to the ball to use a full swing.	3. This is normally caused by running straight at the ball instead of using a slight J-shaped movement to the ball. Also keep your movement smooth and controlled.
4. Opponent cuts off your shots.	4. Hit your shot with more height and more width to make it difficult for your opponent to volley your shot.

MOVING AND HITTING WITHIN THE FRONTCOURT
DRILLS

1. Drives From Front Corner

Stand on the T and throw the ball high into the front corner so that it hits the front wall and side wall, and then bounces on the floor about six feet from the front wall. Run forward and drive the ball into the back corner no farther from the side wall than the width of the service box.

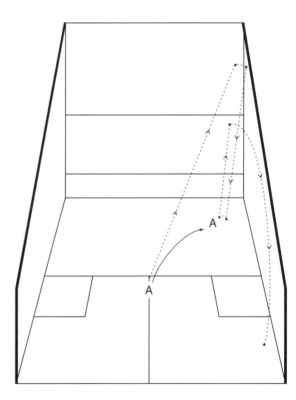

Success Goal =
8 out of 10 forehand drives hitting past the back of the service box ___
8 out of 10 backhand drives hitting past the back of the service box ___

Success Check
• Hit the ball to the side of your front foot ___
• Aim high on the front wall for depth ___
• Keep your back foot still as you swing ___

To Increase Difficulty
• Vary the pace of your drives.
• Throw the ball lower on the front wall.
• Aim at a target in the back corner.

To Decrease Difficulty
• Throw the ball higher on the front wall.
• Move a little closer to the front wall before you throw the ball.

2. Crosscourts From Front Corner

This drill is the same as the first drill except that instead of hitting straight drives, you play a crosscourt drive into the opposite back corner. The ball should hit the opposite side wall behind the short line and then bounce on the floor between the back of the service box and the back wall.

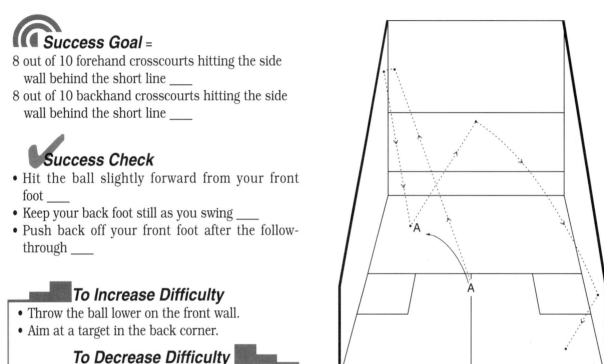

 **Success Goal** =

8 out of 10 forehand crosscourts hitting the side wall behind the short line ___

8 out of 10 backhand crosscourts hitting the side wall behind the short line ___

✔ Success Check

• Hit the ball slightly forward from your front foot ___

• Keep your back foot still as you swing ___

• Push back off your front foot after the follow-through ___

▟ To Increase Difficulty

• Throw the ball lower on the front wall.

• Aim at a target in the back corner.

To Decrease Difficulty ▙

• Throw the ball higher on the front wall.

3. Drives on the Run

Have a partner stand in the back corner and feed short shots to the front of the court. Hit a straight drive to the back corner, turn and run across to touch the opposite side wall, and return to the middle of the court ready for the next shot. Make sure that you turn toward, not away from, the front wall after striking the ball and after touching the side wall. Also, don't hesitate when touching the side wall; return to the T quickly to give yourself plenty of time for the next shot. Your drive should bounce past the back of the service box and no farther than the width of the service box from the side wall.

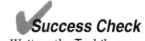 **Success Goal** =

10 consecutive forehand drives past the back of the service box ___

10 consecutive backhand drives past the back of the service box ___

✔ Success Check

• Wait on the T while your partner feeds the ball ___

• Keep your movement as smooth as possible ___

• Push back off your front foot after the follow-through ___

To Increase Difficulty

- Have your partner feed faster and lower so that you must move faster and stretch more for each shot.
- Instead of touching the side wall, turn and play an imaginary shot near the back of the opposite service box.
- Instead of touching the side wall, run backward and touch the back wall between shots.

To Decrease Difficulty

- Have your partner wait longer before feeding the ball so you have plenty of time to move back to the T.
- Have your partner feed the ball higher on the front wall.

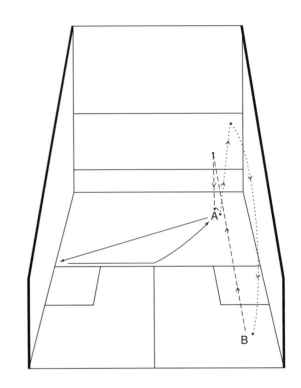

4. Pressure Drives

Stand on the T and have a partner stand in the service box and feed a reverse angle (a shot hitting the opposite side wall before hitting the front wall). The feed should hit the floor after hitting the front wall and then bounce up off the side wall. Run forward to hit a hard straight drive, which the feeder can catch, and then run backward to the T to be ready for the next feed. Try to hit the ball no farther from the side wall than the width of the service box.

Success Goal =

8 out of 10 forehand drives above the tin ___
8 out of 10 backhand drives above the tin ___

Success Check

- Return to the T between shots ___
- Time your movement so that your last step is just before you swing ___
- Keep your body still as you swing ___

To Increase Difficulty

- Have your partner hit low, hard reverse angles.

To Decrease Difficulty

- Have your partner hit reverse angles high on the front wall.

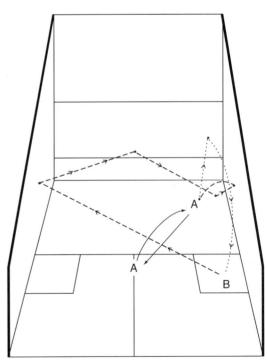

5. Backcourt Versus Frontcourt

This is a conditioned game in which you must hit every shot behind the short line while your opponent must hit every shot in front of the short line. You will serve at the beginning of each point. Use point-per-rally scoring to 9.

**Success Goal** = Win 2 out of 3 games against your opponent ____

✔**Success Check**
- Always watch the ball ____
- Move back to the T after each shot ____
- Hit high on the front wall when under pressure ____

To Increase Difficulty
- Hit everything straight and behind the short line.

To Decrease Difficulty
- Require your opponent to hit everything straight and in front of the short line.
- Require your opponent to hit shots only off the side wall.

6. Two Ball Feeds

This drill requires two feeders, each with a ball, one on the forehand and one on the backhand. They alternate feeding short shots to you. You must move from side to side, hitting straight drives back to the feeders. The feeders should strike the ball in turn, just after you've turned from hitting the last drive. You should make sure that you're turning toward the front wall when moving from side to side and that you turn and watch the ball as the feeder begins the shot. Staring at the front wall will give you less time to set up for your shot and force you to rush too much. As with all drills involving straight drives, try to make the ball bounce behind the back of the service box and no farther from the side wall than the width of the service box.

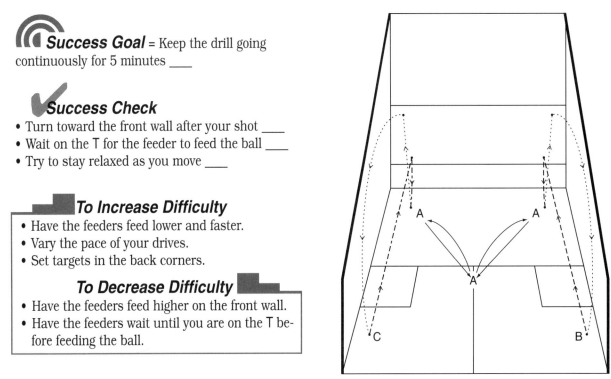

Success Goal = Keep the drill going continuously for 5 minutes ____

✔**Success Check**
- Turn toward the front wall after your shot ____
- Wait on the T for the feeder to feed the ball ____
- Try to stay relaxed as you move ____

To Increase Difficulty
- Have the feeders feed lower and faster.
- Vary the pace of your drives.
- Set targets in the back corners.

To Decrease Difficulty
- Have the feeders feed higher on the front wall.
- Have the feeders wait until you are on the T before feeding the ball.

7. Drives off Short Crosscourts

Player A stands in the back corner and hits a shot that rebounds off the side wall crosscourt to the front wall. Player B stands in the opposite front corner and hits a soft shot across the court into the opposite front corner. You, as player C, have to run forward from the T, hit a straight drive back to player A, and then run backward back to the T. Hit the drive past the back of the service box and no farther from the side wall than the width of the service box. Rather than stopping after each drive player A should keep the drill going by hitting off your drive.

Success Goal =

8 out of 10 forehand drives past the back of the service box ___

8 out of 10 backhand drives past the back of the service box ___

Success Check

- Make a large last step to the ball ___
- Run backward to the T ___
- Keep your eye on the ball ___

To Increase Difficulty

- Have the player at the front hit lower on the front wall.
- Set a target area in the back corner.

To Decrease Difficulty

- Have the player at the front hit higher crosscourt drops.
- Have the player at the back stop before hitting to make sure you have time to recover to the T.

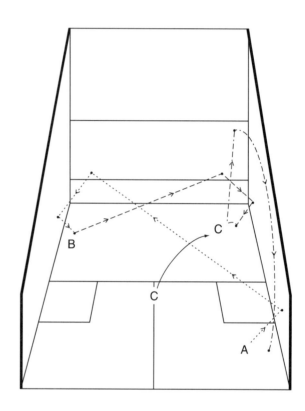

8. Alternating Drives

This is similar to drill 7 except that player B hits straight instead of crosscourt. You must move forward and hit a straight drive; you'll now be alternating between forehand and backhand (see figures a and b). Before moving toward the ball allow player B to step back toward the middle of the court to clear a path for you.

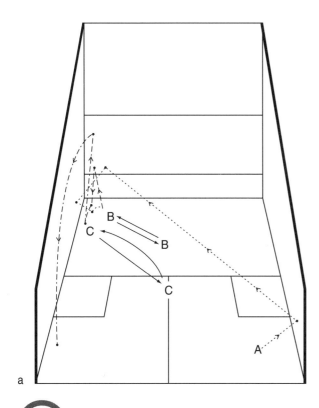

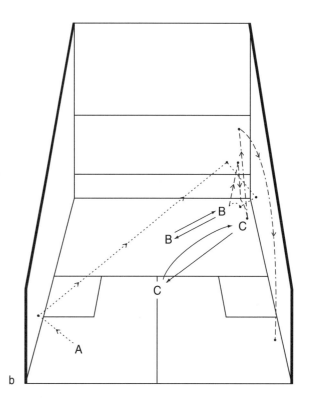

Success Goal = 20 consecutive straight drives without letting the ball bounce twice ___

Success Check

• Prepare your racket early ___
• Bend down low to the ball ___
• Watch the ball as you backpedal to the T ___

To Increase Difficulty

• Allow player B to hit either straight or crosscourt.
• Allow player B any choice of shot at the front, including hitting off the side wall to the front wall.

To Decrease Difficulty

• Have player B hit higher on the front wall to give you more time to reach the shot.

MOVING AND HITTING WITHIN THE FRONTCOURT SUCCESS SUMMARY

The four keys to success when hitting the ball in the frontcourt are the T, balance, keeping your eye on the ball, and J-shaped movement. Be sure you hit with good depth and good width so that you drive your opponent into the back corners rather than allowing your shots to be cut off in midcourt. And remember to backpedal quickly but smoothly to the T after making your shot. Have your coach critique your movement and hitting within the frontcourt using the Keys to Success checklists in figures 4.3 through 4.6.

MOVING AND HITTING WITHIN THE BACKCOURT: DECIDING WHETHER TO USE THE BACK WALL

M ost squash coaches advise you to hit at least 80 percent of your shots to the back corners. Why? Because hitting out of the backcourt is so difficult. If you can keep your opponent pinned there you'll have easy opportunities to win points at the front of the court. It's difficult to hit out of the back corners because the swing is restricted by both the side wall and the back wall.

Remember that while you're trying to pin your opponent in the backcourt, he or she is trying to do the same to you. To hit well out of the back corners, you must maintain good movement and position, know when to strike the ball early and when to wait for it to bounce off the back wall, and have the confidence to bend down and strike the ball close to the floor.

Why Is Moving and Hitting Within the Backcourt Important?

As you play better opponents, you'll find that they will attack you by first driving you deep into the back corners and then looking for opportunities to make you run from the back of the court to the front corners. If you don't develop good movement and hitting out of the backcourt, you'll find yourself hitting weak shots off your opponents' deep shots, which will provide them many easy opportunities to work you up to the front of the court.

How to Move to and From the Back Corners

When moving to the back corners from the T, make sure you don't run straight at the ball (see figure 5.1). Think about trying to stay to the side of the ball as you move back. It's much easier to make a large final step toward the ball just before you hit it than to have to move quickly back to give yourself room to swing. Therefore, your movement in the back corners, like your movement in the front corners, should

Figure 5.1 Use a side-stepping motion to move to a position beside the ball before striking it.

follow a slightly curved route toward the corner rather than a straight line.

After hitting a straight drive from the back you should move behind your opponent and then up the middle of the court to the T (see figure 5.2). However, if you step across and cut off the ball before it reaches the back wall, or if your opponent overhits and the ball rebounds off the back wall back toward the middle of the court, then you may be able to cut straight back to the T without moving behind your opponent. Remember, though, you must give your opponent freedom to move directly to the ball. So if your opponent is trying to move in front of you to the ball and you're in the way, you're probably making the wrong movement back to the T. If you're in doubt about which way your opponent is going to move to the ball, it's best just to concentrate on hitting a tight shot, waiting to see which way your opponent moves, and then going the other way back to the T. Don't rush your shot in order to cut straight to the T. This often leads to a poor shot out from the side wall, which may end up costing you the point. When cut-

ting off the ball, good players often choose to hit a crosscourt shot so they don't risk hitting the ball back to themselves.

How to Hit Within the Backcourt

When hitting out of the back corners it's best to use a midstance (see figure 5.3a and 5.4a). You should turn your body very slightly toward the back corner, but not so far that you to have to flick your wrist to get the ball to go straight down the side wall. Ideally, you'll set up your feet in plenty of time to pause for a second before playing your shot. You still need to transfer your weight onto your front foot just before you strike the ball to get your momentum into the stroke. Sometimes a small step with the front foot will help with this.

Make sure that you keep your racket up high while waiting to play your shot. Try to resist the temptation to drop the racket face down and flick the ball; instead, work on bending your knees and crouching your body down. The midstance should enable you to bend your knees quite a long way and still stay balanced. Give yourself plenty of room from the ball to swing, and turn your front shoulder toward the back corner so you can still generate the power in your shot from the backswing. Stay still while striking the ball and following through, being sure not to move your front foot or your hips. Also, remember to keep your wrist firm and press through the ball as much as possible (see figures 5.3b and 5.4b).

On the follow-through keep your body still and bring your racket face up (see figures 5.3c and 5.4c). Once you have completed the shot push back off your front foot toward the half-court line and then up to the T. Allow your opponent enough room to move in front of you to the ball.

Take a big step with your front foot or step into the corner with your back foot only if you're under pressure and have no time to set up properly. Hitting from this off-balance position is often all you can do. In these situations it's usually best to open the racket face and hit a soft shot high onto the front wall to get the necessary width and depth. Trying to hit too hard normally leads to loss of control. The ball ends up too short and in the middle of the court.

Figure 5.2 Move around the back of your opponent to return to the T.

The better your ability to bend down low and stay balanced, the easier you'll find it to hit shots straight out of the back corners. Sometimes, however, the ball will be too low to hit straight. In this case turn your front shoulder farther around toward the back wall and boast the ball out onto the front wall. A boast is a shot that rebounds off the side wall first before hitting the front wall. Step 8 covers the boast in more depth.

If you step across and cut off a ball before it reaches the back wall, it's often more efficient, especially on the forehand. Note that you must still turn your front shoulder toward the side wall as much as possible. If you have enough time to prepare early and get a good shoulder turn, you can attack the shot and drive it hard, either straight or crosscourt. But if you're rushed or are backing up close to the back wall and can't get a good shoulder turn, it's normally best to open the racket face and hit underneath the ball, placing a high, soft shot straight down the side wall.

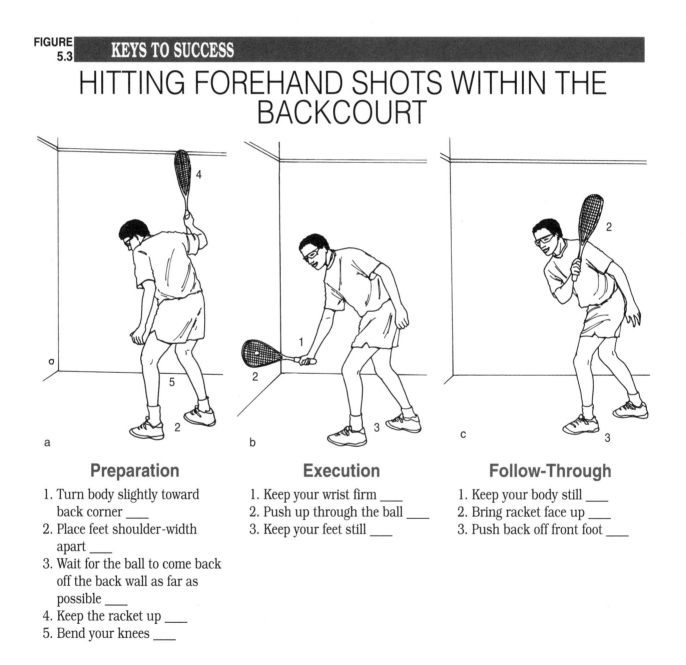

FIGURE 5.3

KEYS TO SUCCESS

HITTING FOREHAND SHOTS WITHIN THE BACKCOURT

Preparation

1. Turn body slightly toward back corner ___
2. Place feet shoulder-width apart ___
3. Wait for the ball to come back off the back wall as far as possible ___
4. Keep the racket up ___
5. Bend your knees ___

Execution

1. Keep your wrist firm ___
2. Push up through the ball ___
3. Keep your feet still ___

Follow-Through

1. Keep your body still ___
2. Bring racket face up ___
3. Push back off front foot ___

FIGURE
5.4

KEYS TO SUCCESS

HITTING BACKHAND SHOTS WITHIN THE BACKCOURT

a

b

Preparation

1. Turn body slightly toward back corner ___
2. Place feet shoulder-width apart ___
3. Wait for the ball to come back off the back wall as far as possible ___
4. Keep the racket up ___
5. Bend your knees ___

Execution

1. Keep your wrist firm ___
2. Push up through the ball ___
3. Keep your feet still ___

Follow-Through

1. Keep your body still ___
2. Bring racket face up ___
3. Push back off front foot ___

c

MOVING AND HITTING WITHIN THE BACKCOURT SUCCESS STOPPERS

Smoothness in your movement and confidence in the way you strike the ball should be your goal when moving and hitting in the backcourt. The following list of errors and corrections will help you achieve this goal.

Error	Correction
1. Too close to ball to use a full swing.	1. Make sure that your first movement from the T is almost directly backward rather than across and then back to the corner.
2. Straight drives hitting side wall before front wall.	2. Make sure that you're standing close to the back wall. Wait for the ball to bounce as far off the back wall as possible. You need to hit the ball out to the side of your front foot.
3. Opponent cuts off your shots.	3. Hit with less power so that you can concentrate on accuracy. If your shot isn't bouncing past the back of the service box, think about trying to hit higher on the front wall.

MOVING AND HITTING IN THE BACKCOURT

DRILLS

1. Drives From the Back Corner

Stand in the back corner about two feet from the back wall and five feet from the side wall. Face the side wall with your racket face up. Throw the ball against the side wall so that it bounces about two feet out from your front foot. Hit a straight drive to the back corner, keeping the ball no farther from the side wall than the width of the service box.

Success Goal =

8 out of 10 forehand drives bouncing beyond the back of the service box ____
8 out of 10 backhand drives bouncing beyond the back of the service box ____

✔ **Success Check**
• Prepare your racket before throwing the ball ___
• Use a midstance ___
• Keep your feet still as you swing ___

To Increase Difficulty
• Set a target in the back corner to aim at.
• Throw the ball against the back wall instead of the side wall.
• Hit crosscourt shots at a target in the opposite back corner.

To Decrease Difficulty
• Stand farther forward in the court.

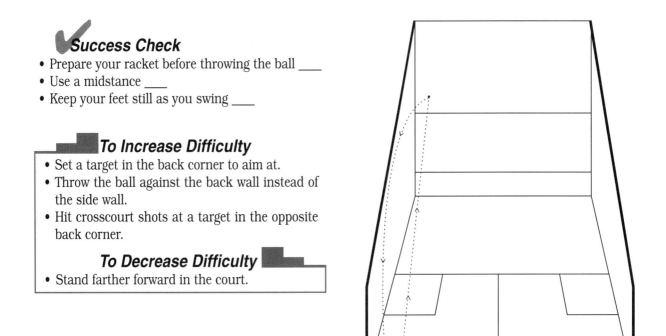

2. Continuous Drives

This is similar to drill 1, except this time try to hit continuous drives, keeping a rally going with yourself as long you can. Try to make all your shots hit the floor and then the back wall, although be prepared to step in early to hit the ball if you think it's going to die before it hits the back wall. Once the ball has hit the back wall wait for it to rebound as far from the back wall as possible before striking it. If you overhit a drive so that it bounces off the back wall before hitting the floor, take much of the pace off your next shot because the momentum of the ball flying off the back wall makes it easy to overhit the second shot as well.

Success Goal = 10 continuous drives ___

✔ **Success Check**
• Wait for the ball to drop before striking it ___
• Bend your knees ___
• Aim high on the front wall ___

To Increase Difficulty
• Vary the pace of your shots.
• Hit three straight drives and then a crosscourt.
• Set a smaller target area to aim at.

To Decrease Difficulty
• Let the ball bounce a second time after it has hit the back wall.
• Keep a rally going by hitting softer shots that don't hit the back wall.

3. Backcourt Drives on the Run

Have a partner stand on the T and feed you a straight drive to the back corner. Hit a straight drive from the back, aiming the ball to hit above the cut line and staying within a service-box width of the side wall. Then turn, move across, and touch the opposite side wall before returning to the back corner ready for the next feed. The feeder should try to stop the ball before it passes so that he or she can quickly feed the next drive.

Success Goal =

20 consecutive forehand drives hit above the cut line ___

20 consecutive backhand drives hit above the cut line ___

Success Check

• Finish your follow-through before turning to move toward the side wall ___
• Turn toward the front wall ___
• Give yourself plenty of room to hit ___

To Increase Difficulty

• Run forward and across, touching the side wall in front of the opposite service box between shots.
• Have your partner feed as quickly as possible.

To Decrease Difficulty

• Have your partner wait for you to get back in position before feeding the ball.

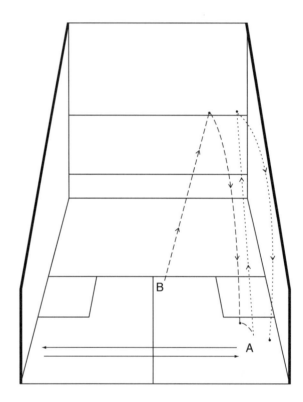

4. Backcourt Rallying

With a partner, play a rally in the back corner, hitting only straight drives. Make sure that you circle around each other. After you have struck the ball move behind your partner to the T. Avoid becoming stuck in the back corner while your opponent stands in front cutting off all your shots; be sure your shots are deep into the backcourt and close to the side wall. Make sure that you prepare your racket smoothly, because whipping it back too quickly may endanger your opponent.

Success Goal =

5 minutes of continuous rallying on the forehand ___

5 minutes of continuous rallying on the backhand ___

Success Check

• Always keep your eye on the ball ___
• Concentrate on accuracy rather than power ___
• Circle around your partner ___

To Increase Difficulty

- Set target areas; for example, all shots must bounce behind the back of the service box and no farther from the side wall than the width of the service box.
- Play a conditioned game; the first person to miss the target area loses the point. (If you and your partner are of different ability, establish a smaller area for the better player to aim at.)

To Decrease Difficulty

- If necessary, allow the ball to bounce more than once to keep the rally going.

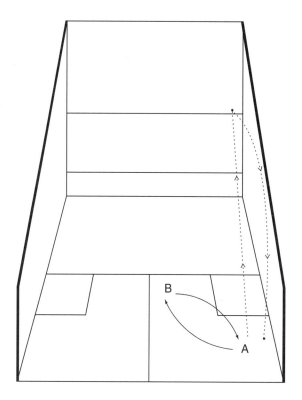

5. Backcourt Game

Play a conditioned game in which you and your opponent must hit shots that bounce past the short line. Play the game with point-per-rally scoring to 9 points.

Success Goal = Win 2 out of 3 games from your opponent ___

Success Check

- Intercept shots that may die in the back corners ___
- Hit high on the front wall when under pressure ___
- Hit with good width and depth to stop your opponent from cutting off your shots ___

To Increase Difficulty

- Allow your opponent to hit any shot, but you must hit your shots past the short line.

To Decrease Difficulty

- Allow one shot per player per rally to bounce in front of the short line.

6. Two Ball Feeds

Have two feeders, each with a ball, stand on the short line and feed alternate straight drives on the forehand and backhand sides. You must stand at the back of the court and move from side to side hitting straight drives.

Success Goal = Hit drives continuously for 5 minutes ___

Success Check
- Hit the ball with your body turned slightly toward the back corner ___
- Keep your hips still as you swing ___
- Move smoothly across the court ___

To Increase Difficulty
- Have one feeder hit a straight drive and the other hit a straight drop (a short shot to the frontcourt). Run diagonally across the court, between the feeders, and hit a straight drive from the back and then a straight drive from the front.

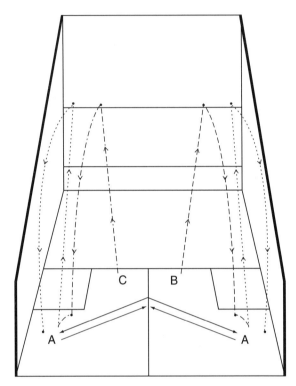

MOVING AND HITTING WITHIN THE BACKCOURT SUCCESS SUMMARY

Hitting in the backcourt is without doubt the toughest aspect of the game. To give yourself good position you should either wait for the ball to bounce as far off the back wall as possible or cut it off before it hits the back wall. By mastering this area of the court, you'll limit your opponent's main means of attack. Ask another player to evaluate your skills in moving and hitting within the backcourt using the Keys to Success checklists in figures 5.3 and 5.4.

STEP 6
THE VOLLEY: TAKING THE INITIATIVE

Volleying is one of the most important elements of squash. When players step up and take the ball on the volley, they speed up the game and stretch their opponents to the limit. A good volleyer dominates the T, punishing any shot that the opponent doesn't hit tight to the side walls.

The volley is a shot hit before the ball bounces on the floor. Players often use the volley around the middle of the court to cut off an opponent's shot before it reaches the back. It can also be hit from the back of the court off an opponent's soft, high shot or on the return of serve.

To begin with, work on hitting your volleys deep into the back of the court because this is a higher percentage shot than a volley to the front of the court. As your volleying becomes more consistent you'll want to vary your volley more and hit some volley drops and kills. Steps 9 and 10 cover these shots.

Whenever possible you should hit an attacking volley with plenty of pace and good width and depth. This will put your opponent under pressure and keep the advantage you've gained by taking the ball early. It will sometimes be necessary, however, to hit a soft, high defensive volley with the sole aim of maneuvering your opponent into one of the back corners.

Why Is the Volley Important?

Volleying is important for several reasons. First, taking the ball on the volley often helps you avoid playing more difficult shots from the back of the court. It also saves energy, cutting down on the running you have to do to retrieve the ball from the back of the court. Moreover, it helps reduce the time your opponent has to recover after hitting a shot. The last reason is probably the most important, especially as you become better at handling shots from the back corners. In tight matches, the player who steps up

and takes the initiative by volleying often comes out on top.

How to Perform the Forehand Volley

Preparation is important with the volley. You need time to concentrate on the way you strike the ball. While waiting for your opponent's shot keep your racket face up rather than down by your feet. Then, when your opponent strikes the ball and you see the direction it's going, bring your racket back to be ready for your shot (see figure 6.1a). Keep your wrist cocked and your elbow slightly bent. Use a slightly shorter backswing than you use for the forehand drive so you can hit the ball with more control. Step across with your front foot and turn your front shoulder toward the side wall.

Strike the ball level with your front shoulder when hitting a straight volley and slightly farther forward for a crosscourt volley. Keep your wrist firm and punch or push through the ball (see figure 6.1b). As with the drive you should hit with an open racket face to help you hit high enough on the front wall to get the ball to the back of the court.

Follow through in the intended direction of your shot (see figure 6.1c). Use a more compact follow-through than the one you use for the forehand drive. Also, make sure that you keep your hips and feet still until you've finished the shot.

You'll find that you don't always have time to step across on the front foot for the forehand volley. It's perfectly acceptable in this situation to hit the ball off the back, or "wrong," foot. Make sure, however, that you turn your front shoulder so that your shoulders are parallel to the side wall. Avoid hitting with your chest facing the front wall because this will cause you to drag the ball down toward the tin.

59

FIGURE
6.1   **KEYS TO SUCCESS**

FOREHAND VOLLEY

Preparation

1. Bring racket back early ___
2. Turn your shoulders ___
3. Use a short backswing ___
4. Keep wrist cocked ___
5. Keep elbow bent ___
6. Step across on front foot ___

Execution

1. Keep wrist firm and cocked ___
2. Strike the ball level with front shoulder ___
3. Punch through the ball ___

Follow-Through

1. Keep your feet still ___
2. Keep your hips still ___
3. Follow through in the intended direction of your shot ___

How to Perform the Backhand Volley

Early preparation is just as important for the backhand volley as it is for the forehand volley. Bring your wrist up so that your racket face goes behind the back of your head (see figure 6.2a). Keep your wrist cocked and your knuckles facing up. Step across on your front foot and turn your front shoulder toward the side wall.

Strike the ball slightly farther forward than your front shoulder with your racket face open (see figure 6.2b). Your wrist should stay firm throughout the shot, and you should punch through the ball. As with the forehand, when hitting crosscourt take the ball early, striking it even farther forward of your front shoulder.

Keep the follow-through more compact than you do when hitting the backhand drive, but bring the racket face up in a similar manner (see figure 6.2c). Your hips and feet should stay still until you've finished the shot.

FIGURE 6.2

KEYS TO SUCCESS

BACKHAND VOLLEY

a   b   c

Preparation

1. Keep racket face behind head ___
2. Cock your wrist ___
3. Keep knuckles facing up ___
4. Turn front shoulder toward side wall ___
5. Step across on front foot ___

Execution

1. Keep wrist firm ___
2. Hold racket face open ___
3. Make contact slightly farther forward than your front shoulder ___
4. Punch through the ball ___

Follow-Through

1. Keep your feet still ___
2. Keep your hips still ___
3. Follow through in the intended direction of your shot ___

How to Volley From Deep in the Court

You must often hit a volley from near the back wall, usually following an opponent's serve or lob shot. If you don't volley in this situation the ball will often die in the back corner, giving you no chance to return it. Generally, the deeper you are in the court, the more defensive your volley should be. Concentrate on turning sideways (see figures 6.3a and 6.4a) and punching through the ball. Make sure you bend your knees slightly for balance and watch the ball carefully onto the racket face (see figures 6.3b and 6.4b). Remember that the power comes from the backswing, not from throwing your body into the shot. So keep your body and feet still and control your follow-through as well as you can (see figures 6.3c and 6.4c). Finally, give yourself plenty of room to swing, particularly if you're volleying the ball after it has hit the side wall.

FIGURE 6.3

KEYS TO SUCCESS

FOREHAND VOLLEY FROM DEEP IN THE COURT

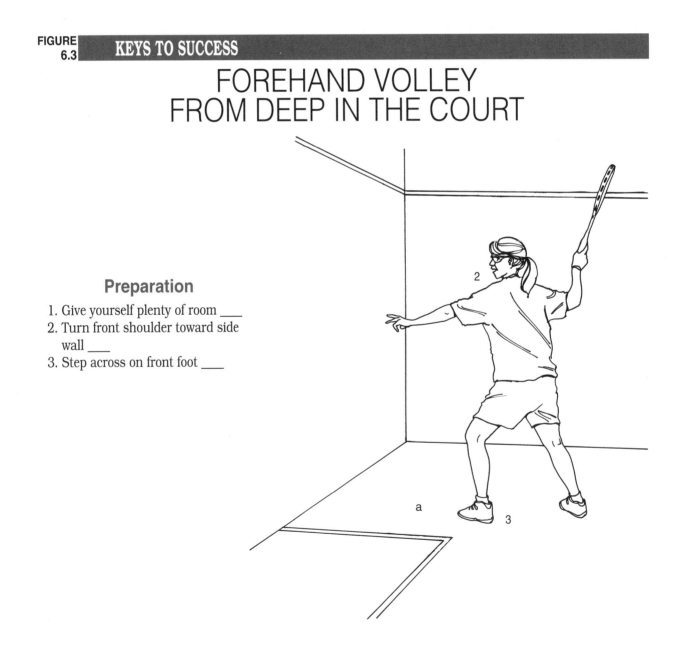

Preparation

1. Give yourself plenty of room ___
2. Turn front shoulder toward side wall ___
3. Step across on front foot ___

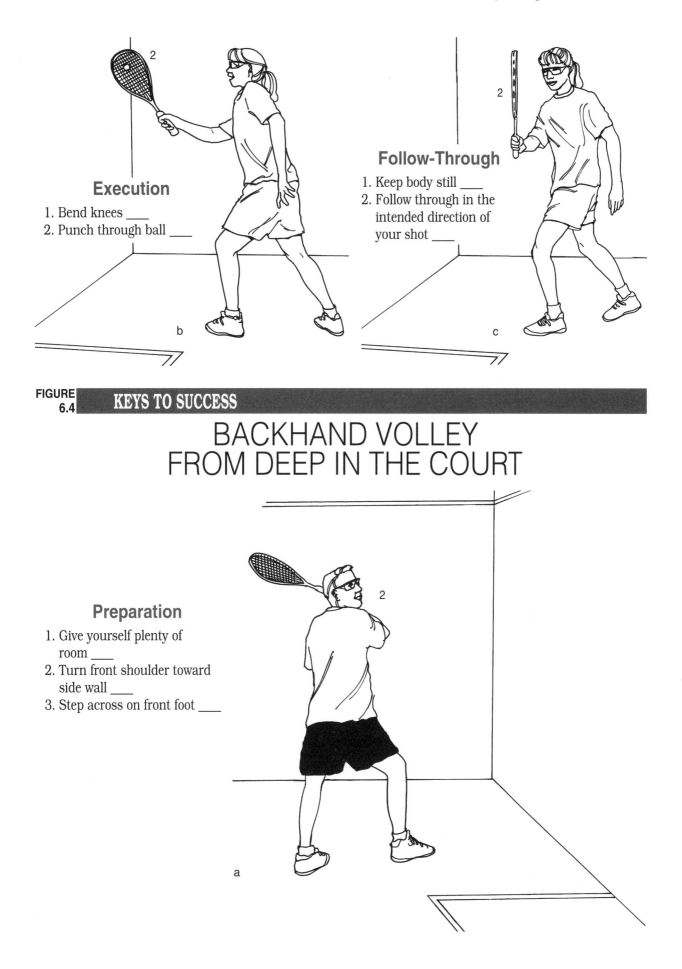

Execution

1. Bend knees ___
2. Punch through ball ___

b

Follow-Through

1. Keep body still ___
2. Follow through in the intended direction of your shot ___

c

FIGURE 6.4 **KEYS TO SUCCESS**

BACKHAND VOLLEY FROM DEEP IN THE COURT

Preparation

1. Give yourself plenty of room ___
2. Turn front shoulder toward side wall ___
3. Step across on front foot ___

a

Execution

1. Bend knees ___
2. Punch through ball ___

b

Follow-Through

1. Keep body still ___
2. Follow through in the
   intended direction of
   your shot ___

c

VOLLEY SUCCESS STOPPERS

To be a good volleyer you need to have the confidence to step across quickly and take the ball early. Most problems with the volley come from not preparing the racket fast enough. The following list of corrections to common errors on the volley should help you with the shot, giving you the confidence to react quickly and take every opportunity to volley.

Error	Correction
1. No time to hit a volley.	1. Watch carefully as your opponent hits the ball and prepare your racket early.
2. Volley lacks power.	2. Grip the racket a bit more firmly and keep your wrist firm as you push through the shot.
3. Volley lacks depth.	3. Open the racket face more so that you can hit higher on the front wall. Also keep your wrist firm.
4. Straight volley goes down the middle of the court.	4. This is probably caused by hitting too soon. Wait for the ball to come to the side of your body.
5. Mis-hitting the volley.	5. Make sure that you watch the ball carefully onto the racket face.
6. Volley lacks control.	6. Keep your body still as you strike the ball and try using a shorter swing.

VOLLEY

DRILLS

1. Target Volleys

Set a target against the side wall about two feet behind the back of the service box. Stand on the short line about six feet from the side wall. Hit a soft feed about halfway up the front wall. Volley the ball straight into the back corner. Try to make your volley bounce on the target.

Success Goal =
5 out of 10 forehand volleys hitting the target ____
5 out of 10 backhand volleys hitting the target ____

Success Check
• Prepare your racket early ____
• Keep your wrist firm ____
• Punch through the ball ____

To Increase Difficulty
• Move farther back in the court.
• Hit crosscourt volleys to a target in the opposite back corner.

To Decrease Difficulty
• Move forward in the court.

2. Continuous Volleys

Stand on the short line and continually volley the ball back to yourself. Keep on the balls of your feet and adjust your feet constantly to position yourself correctly for each volley.

Success Goal =
20 consecutive forehand volleys ____
20 consecutive backhand volleys ____

Success Check
• Prepare your racket quickly ____
• Keep your body still as you swing ____
• Use a short swing ____

To Increase Difficulty
• Move farther back in the court.
• Alternate forehand and backhand volleys.

To Decrease Difficulty
• Move forward in the court.

3. Front Corner Crisscross Volleys

Stand on the T. Hit a forehand across your body so that it hits the front wall close to the side wall. The ball should rebound off the side wall back to the middle of the court. Then hit a backhand volley to the opposite front corner so that it hits the front wall, then the side wall, and then returns to the middle. Keep this going as long as you can without the ball hitting the floor.

**Success Goal =** 20 consecutive volleys ____

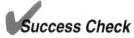**Success Check**

- Turn your shoulder as you prepare your racket ___
- Hit the shot on the front wall close to the side wall ___
- Shuffle your feet to get into the correct position to hit ___

To Increase Difficulty
- Move farther forward in the court.

To Decrease Difficulty
- Let the ball hit the floor to get into a rhythm.

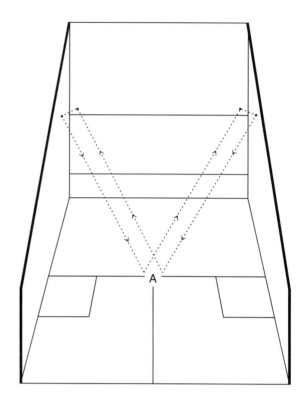

4. Volley From Partner's Feed

Have a partner stand in the back corner and feed soft, high shots. Step across from the T and hit straight volleys. If possible your partner should keep the exercise going without stopping between shots. Try to make the volleys bounce behind the back of the service box and no farther from the side wall than the width of the service box.

Success Goal =

8 out of 10 forehand volleys bouncing behind short line ___
8 out of 10 backhand volleys bouncing behind short line ___

Success Check

- Step across with your front foot ___
- Transfer your weight to the front foot as you hit ___
- Hit the ball between your body and the side wall ___

To Increase Difficulty
- Set a target in the back corner to aim at.
- Have your partner stand farther forward and volley your shots.

To Decrease Difficulty
- Have your partner stop after each shot so that you have time to prepare for the next one.

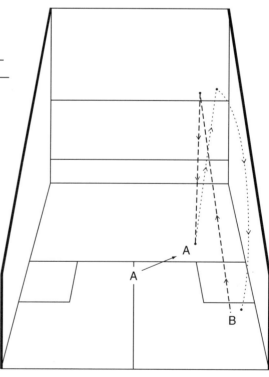

5. Volleys on the Run

From a partner's soft, high feed, hit a volley. The volley should bounce behind the back of the service box and no farther from the side wall than the width of the service box. Then turn and run across to touch the opposite side wall before returning to the T for the next volley.

Success Goal =

8 out of 10 forehand volleys bouncing behind the back of the service box ____

8 out of 10 backhand volleys bouncing behind the back of the service box ____

Success Check

• Watch your partner strike the ball ____
• Time your movement so that your last step is just before you swing ____
• Keep your body still as you punch through ____

To Increase Difficulty

• Have your partner feed faster and lower to make you stretch more and move more quickly.
• Instead of touching the side wall, play an imaginary shot close to the back of the opposite service box.
• Instead of touching the side wall, run backward and touch the back wall between shots.

To Decrease Difficulty

• Have your partner wait for you to return to the T before feeding the ball.

6. Two Ball Feeds for Volleys

Have two feeders, each with a ball, alternate feeding shots for you to volley, one on the forehand and one on the backhand. Move from side to side, hitting straight volleys back to the feeders. The feeder should strike the ball just after you have turned from hitting the last volley. As with all volley drills, try to make the ball bounce behind the back of the service box and no farther from the side wall than the width of the service box.

Success Goal = 5 minutes of continuous volleying ____

Success Check

• Turn toward the front wall after each volley ____
• Prepare your racket early ____
• Wait on the T for the feeder to feed the ball ____

To Increase Difficulty

• Have the feeders feed lower and faster.

To Decrease Difficulty

• Have the feeders wait longer before feeding the ball.

7. Crosscourt Cutoffs

Player A stands in a back corner and hits the ball off the side wall to the opposite frontcourt. Player B stands in the opposite front corner and hits a crosscourt drive. You, as player C, stand on the T and cut off the crosscourt with a straight volley back to player A.

**Success Goal** = Keep drill going for 5 minutes ____

 **Success Check**

- Step across on front foot ___
- Hit volley between body and the side wall ___
- Keep your wrist firm ___

To Increase Difficulty

- Have player B vary the pace, width, and height of the crosscourts.

To Decrease Difficulty

- Have player B hit soft crosscourts to make volley easier.

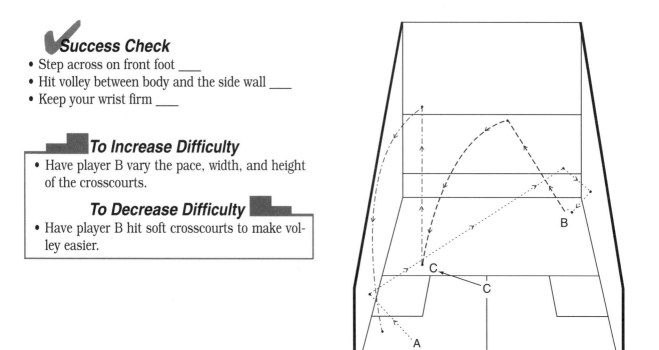

8. Random Cutoffs

This drill is similar to drill 7, except player B, at the front of the court, has the option of hitting either crosscourts or straight drives. You must watch carefully and be ready to volley on either your forehand or backhand side.

Success Goal = Keep drill going for 3 minutes ___

Success Check

- Watch the ball carefully ___
- Prepare racket quickly ___
- Punch the ball ___

To Increase Difficulty

- Have player B vary the pace and height of the straight and crosscourt drives.

To Decrease Difficulty

- Have player B alternate between hitting straight and crosscourt drives.

VOLLEY SUCCESS SUMMARY

When you use it well, the volley speeds up the pace of the match, stretching your opponent to the limit and allowing little time to recover from the previous shot. In tight matches it's often the key to victory. In addition, the volley helps you avoid more difficult shots out of the back corners, a huge plus for lower-level players. Have a friend check your volley against the Keys to Success checklists in figures 6.1 through 6.4.

STEP 7

SERVE AND RETURN OF SERVE: CONTROLLING THE RALLY

When top players serve they appear to be putting almost no thought or effort into the shot. Unlike in tennis, the serve rarely wins the point immediately, and thus its importance seems limited. Actually though, the serve is often crucial to success in a match. Top players develop a basic serve that they are confident will pressure their opponent. They add to this by perfecting variations of serve to keep their opponents on their toes and unsure of what to expect.

The way you return the serve often sets the tone for the rally. If you attack the serve with a shot to the frontcourt, the server will often counterattack. The ensuing rally will usually be short, with many attempted "winners." A defensive shot to the back corners will often lead to a longer, drawn-out rally. Therefore, you can use the return of serve to set a tone for the rally that is right for you.

Why Is the Serve Important?

It's important to take advantage of the serve because it's the only shot you don't have to move for to hit. A good serve puts your opponent on the defensive and allows you to control the T immediately. A weak serve, however, gives your opponent the opportunity to attack and take the initiative from you.

How to Serve From the Left Box

The basic serve from the left box (right box for left-handed players) is similar to the basic forehand drive. You should begin by facing the opposite side wall with your back foot completely in the box and your racket up ready to hit a forehand (see figure 7.1a). Step across with your front foot while throwing the ball toward the opposite side wall. Be careful not to throw the ball too high because this will make timing the swing difficult. Also be sure to throw the ball about three or four feet away from your body so that you aren't cramped when swinging. A good way of approaching this is to stretch your arm out fully and just let the ball roll off your fingers.

Remember that when you serve you must strike the ball before it bounces. As you step across to hit, turn your front shoulder slightly toward the opposite back corner and let the ball drop to between waist and knee height before swinging (see figure 7.1b). Swing as you do for the forehand drive, keeping the wrist cocked and pushing through the ball. Control your swing and don't try to hit the ball too hard. You'll only waste energy and hit a less accurate shot. After you have struck the ball, move smoothly to the T, keeping your eye on the ball as it travels toward the back corner (see figure 7.1c).

Aim your serve slightly to the right of the center on the front wall, about two-thirds of the way up. More important, though, the ball should hit the side wall toward the back of the service box at about the point where your opponent would try to cut it off (see figure 7.2). Make sure you hit the ball hard enough and high enough that it bounces on the floor close to the back wall. Ideally, your serve should be too difficult for your opponent to hit straight, and should force a return off the side wall to the frontcourt. Make sure that you keep your wrist firm and your body still as you swing through. Too much movement with your hips will make you hit the ball too high and to the right, causing the ball to go out of court on the side wall.

FIGURE 7.1

KEYS TO SUCCESS

BASIC SERVE FROM THE LEFT BOX

Preparation

1. Face opposite side wall ___
2. Keep back foot in box ___
3. Hold racket up ready for a forehand ___

Execution

1. Step across with front foot ___
2. Throw the ball out toward the T ___
3. Let the ball drop to waist height ___
4. Keep wrist firm ___
5. Keep hips still ___

Follow-Through

1. Step toward the T ___
2. Watch the ball ___

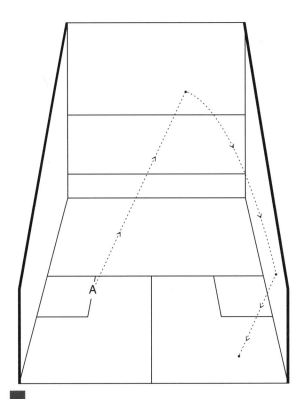

Figure 7.2 Ball path for the serve from the left box.

How to Serve From the Right Box

For the right side (the left side for left-handers), two serves will be described—a basic serve and a more advanced serve, which you should start to work on when you're comfortable with the basic serve. You should begin by facing the side wall nearest you with your back foot in the box and, again, your racket prepared for a forehand (see figure 7.3a on page 72). This time throw the ball out to your side but slightly

forward from your body so that you'll contact the ball in front of you. As you throw, take a small step forward with your front foot, let the ball drop again to between waist and knee height, and then swing through (see figure 7.3b on page 72). Again, keep your wrist firm and body still. Think also about hitting underneath the ball to get some height on the shot. Immediately after you've struck the ball begin to move to the T (see figure 7.3c on page 72). The ball should hit the center of the front wall about two-thirds of the way up so that it hits the side wall toward the back of the service box (see figure 7.4).

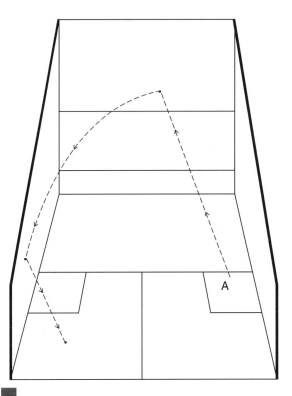

Figure 7.4 Ball path for the serve from the right box.

FIGURE 7.3

KEYS TO SUCCESS

BASIC SERVE FROM THE RIGHT BOX

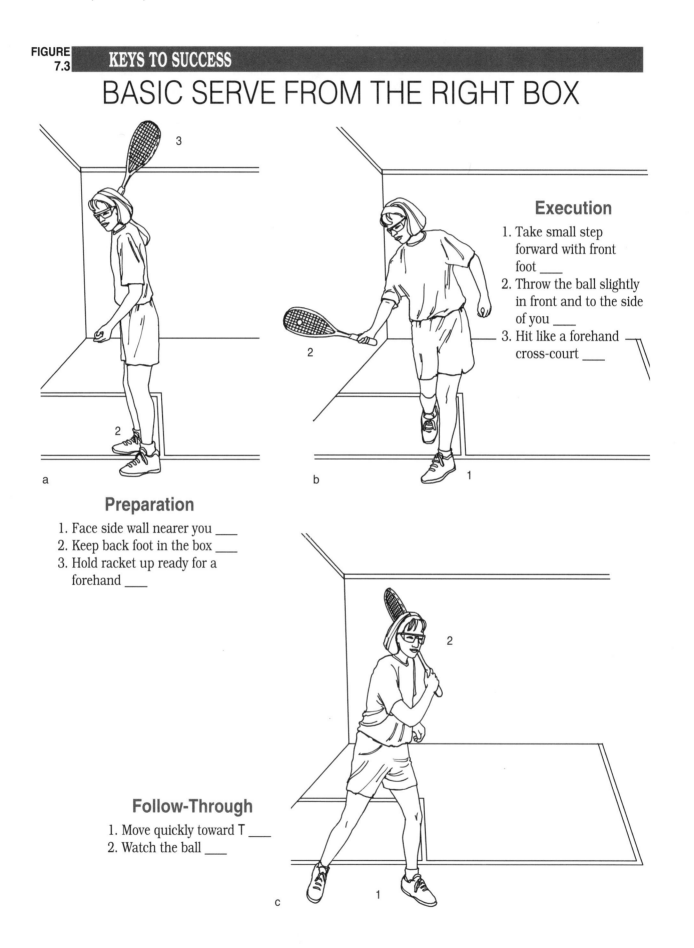

Execution

1. Take small step forward with front foot ___
2. Throw the ball slightly in front and to the side of you ___
3. Hit like a forehand cross-court ___

Preparation

1. Face side wall nearer you ___
2. Keep back foot in the box ___
3. Hold racket up ready for a forehand ___

Follow-Through

1. Move quickly toward T ___
2. Watch the ball ___

ADVANCED SERVE FROM THE RIGHT BOX

With some practice you can usually hit a reasonably consistent tight serve with the basic serve from the right box. The basic serve has some problems, however, the biggest of which is that stepping forward means that your momentum is not going toward the T. You must, therefore, move quickly toward the middle so that you're in position when your opponent returns the serve. An improvement on the basic serve would be to step across toward the T with the front foot and turn the body to an open position instead of stepping forward. Start in the same position as for the basic serve (see figure 7.5a), but then throw the ball more to the side of your body. Drag the ball across the court with the momentum of your body as you move toward the T (see figure 7.5b). This difficult motion requires plenty of practice. It's often best to work at it in stages. To begin with, stand in an open position with your body facing the front wall. Work only on throwing the ball up to the side of yourself and hitting it toward the center of the front wall. Transferring the weight from your back foot to your front foot as you do this will help keep your body movement smooth throughout the shot.

FIGURE 7.5 **KEYS TO SUCCESS**

ADVANCED SERVE FROM THE RIGHT BOX

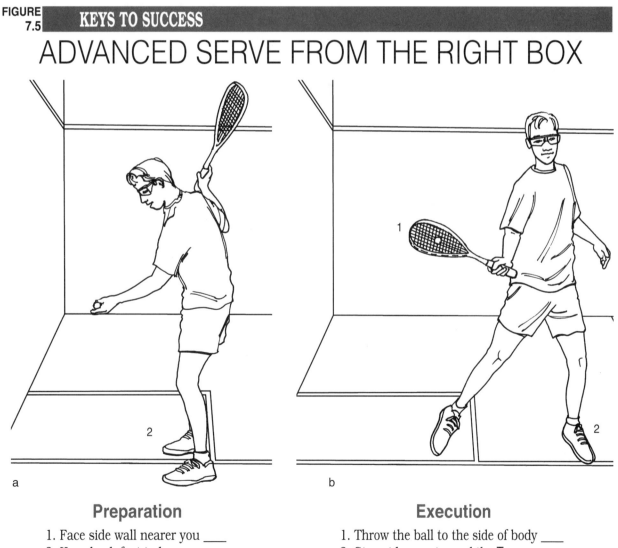

a   b

Preparation
1. Face side wall nearer you ___
2. Keep back foot in box ___

Execution
1. Throw the ball to the side of body ___
2. Step sideways toward the T ___

Varying the Serve

The serves described in the previous sections are stock serves that you'll use about 75 percent of the time. You should work hard on them to develop consistency. Keep in mind, however, that it may be advantageous to adapt your stock serve according to how your opponent is dealing with it. If your opponent is stepping forward and volleying your serve before it hits the side wall, aim farther across the front wall to make sure the ball hits the side wall first. This will make attacking your serve much harder. On the other hand, if your opponent makes few attempts to volley your serve and instead lets most of them go to the back, then you should adjust your aim to make the ball hit the side closer to the back corner. This will increase your chances of the ball taking an awkward bounce out of one of the nicks (cracks between walls and floor).

Besides your stock serve, you should have some variations to throw in occasionally to keep your opponent guessing.

Lob Serve

Use a motion similar to that of your stock serve but hit with less power and hit more underneath the ball to lift it high on the front wall. You should use a slightly shorter backswing for more control. Bend your knees a little more than you do on your stock serve (see figure 7.6a). Aim your shot to hit high in the center of the front wall (see figure 7.6b). The ball should hit on the side wall a couple of feet below the out-of-court line and at about the back of the service box. The object of the lob serve is to force your opponent to hit a difficult high volley. This serve carries a substantial risk of serving out, however, so use it sparingly.

FIGURE 7.6

KEYS TO SUCCESS

LOB SERVE

Preparation

1. Stand in the same position as for the stock serve ___
2. Use a short backswing ___
3. Bend your knees ___

Execution

1. Throw and step in the same way as for the stock serve ___
2. Hit underneath the ball ___
3. Hit with less pace ___
4. Aim high on the front wall ___

Hard-Hit Serve

Again, use a motion similar to that which you use for your stock serve but this time swing through faster and hit a little lower on the front wall (see figure 7.7a). It sometimes helps to strike the ball a little higher in the air as well (see figure 7.7b). This serve is particularly effective when directed down the middle of the court straight at your opponent's body. The object of the hard-hit serve is to surprise your opponent and force a rushed return from an off-balance position. Don't overuse this shot or you'll lose the element of surprise.

FIGURE 7.7

KEYS TO SUCCESS

HARD-HIT SERVE

a

b

Preparation

1. Stand in same position as for the stock serve ___
2. Keep racket up high ___
3. Throw ball slightly higher than stock serve ___

Execution

1. Step in the same way as for the stock serve ___
2. Strike the ball higher in the air ___
3. Swing through quickly ___
4. Hit lower on the front wall ___
5. Aim shot down the middle of the court ___

Backhand Serve

This is useful from the right box but has very few advantages from the left box. From the right it changes the angle of the serve, often making it easier to keep the ball close to the side wall. It also allows you to see where your opponent is standing for the return and enables you to move smoothly and quickly to the T. Execute the serve similar to the way you perform a forehand serve from the left side. Begin by facing the opposite side wall with your racket prepared for a backhand (see figure 7.8a). Throw the ball out to the side of you, cross your left arm under your right arm, and step across the court with your front foot. Turn your front shoulder toward the back corner so that you can get some power in the shot from the backswing. Hit the ball in a similar manner to the way you hit a backhand drive (see figure 7.8b).

FIGURE 7.8

KEYS TO SUCCESS

BACKHAND SERVE (FROM RIGHT BOX)

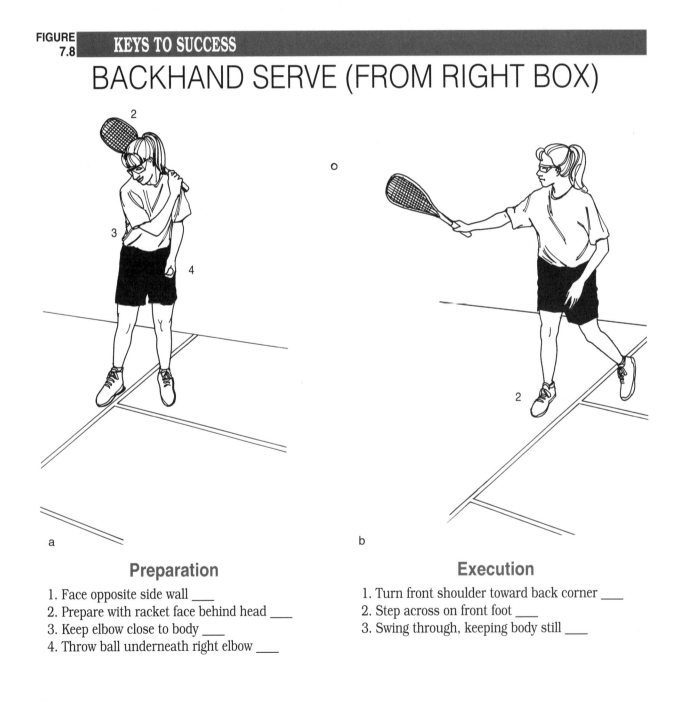

a

b

Preparation

1. Face opposite side wall ___
2. Prepare with racket face behind head ___
3. Keep elbow close to body ___
4. Throw ball underneath right elbow ___

Execution

1. Turn front shoulder toward back corner ___
2. Step across on front foot ___
3. Swing through, keeping body still ___

Why Is the Return of Serve Important?

A strong return of serve is crucial in gaining the center of the court and taking the initiative from the server. At lower levels, where rallies tend to be much shorter, the first few shots in a rally often dictate how the rally is going to be played out. For example, the first player to hit a tight shot to the back of the court often wins the rally immediately or is set up for a winning shot by the opponent's weak return. As your level of play improves you'll find that it becomes increasingly difficult to win a rally with one good shot, and that a combination of good shots is necessary. Still, the return of serve is important because it may be the only shot in the rally for which you have plenty of time to prepare. It's a good opportunity to begin the series of good shots necessary to win the rally.

Return of Serve Options

When returning the serve you have three basic options. You can go for an attacking shot at the front of the court, hit more defensively into the back corner, or boast the ball to the front of the court (see step 8). The first option is a low-percentage option. You should play it only if the serve is very weak or if you're feeling particularly confident with your attacking shot. The second option is normally preferable, but if this isn't possible because the serve was very good, the last option may be the only way to keep the ball in play.

So most of the time you should be looking to hit to the back corners. Try to volley the serve straight down the wall, either before or after the ball has hit the side wall. The only exception to this is if the serve is overhit and you're confident it will bounce a long way off the back wall. In this case, waiting is often better because it gives you time to set up and thus choose from many options. If the serve is overhit to such a degree that the ball hits the side wall and then the back wall before hitting the floor, give yourself plenty of room to hit your shot. The ball is likely to move a long way out into the middle of the court, so you should back up, forcing your opponent back and giving you a wide lane to hit a straight drive into the back corner.

If you're poorly positioned to hit the ball straight, particularly if you step forward to hit a volley but end up where you're hitting the ball in front of yourself, it's best to hit a deep crosscourt shot. Attempting to hit the volley straight normally leads to a poor return that often comes straight back to you. Make sure your crosscourt return is high and wide enough so that your opponent can't easily volley. Again, aim to hit the opposite side wall near the back of the service box.

How to Perform the Return of Serve

When you're waiting to return the serve, it's best to stand slightly behind and to the side of the service box opposite the server. Have your racket up ready for a forehand on the forehand side (see figure 7.9) or a backhand on the backhand side (see figure 7.10).

Figure 7.9 Forehand return of serve waiting position.

Figure 7.10 Backhand return of serve waiting position.

Turn your head and watch the ball as your opponent serves.

As the ball hits the front wall begin to turn your body to a more sideways position and extend your racket back even farther. Shuffle your feet to get into the best position to strike the ball. Be sure to give yourself enough room to swing through comfortably. Hit the ball to the side of your body, keeping your wrist firm as you swing through.

Follow through in the direction you want the ball to go. Your hips and feet should stay still until you have finished the follow-through. Once you've completed the stroke move smoothly to the T. Give your opponent room to move in front of you to the back corner if you've hit the ball deep and straight.

SERVE AND RETURN OF SERVE SUCCESS STOPPERS

To use the serve as a weapon you must be able to make constant adjustments. Try to remember the following list of adjustments each time you step on court. Most of the problems with the return of serve are caused by either rushing or trying to be too aggressive with the shot. If you're having trouble with this aspect of your game, be patient and think about just making a solid return that will keep you in the rally.

Error	Correction
1. Serve not reaching short line.	1. Step into the serve to get more power. Let the ball drop lower so that you can use a full swing.
2. Serve goes out of court.	2. Hit the serve with less power and aim lower on the front wall.
3. Opponent cuts off serve with an attacking volley.	3. Make sure that your serve hits the side wall. Alternatively, this is the ideal time to use a hard serve down the middle of the court.
4. Opponent's serve is dying in the back corner.	4. Make every effort to volley the serve.
5. Return of serve goes down the middle of the court.	5. Be sure to make up your mind early whether to hit straight or crosscourt. If you're hitting crosscourt, hit with more width. If you're hitting straight, make sure that you hit your shot to the side of your body.

SERVE AND RETURN OF SERVE

DRILLS

1. Throw and Hit

The purpose of this drill is to practice the motion of throwing and hitting the ball before it bounces without having to worry about where you are standing or aiming the shot. Stand in the middle of the court. Throw the ball in the air about three to four feet from your body and hit it against the front wall. You should let the ball drop to about waist height before making contact, and you should hit the ball with a forehand swing. Aim to hit your shot high on the center of the front wall.

 *Success Goal* = 10 consecutive hits against the front wall ___

✔ *Success Check*
• Use a forehand swing ___
• Let the ball drop to waist height ___
• Watch the ball onto racket face ___

To Increase Difficulty
• Aim your shots to hit above the cut line and bounce past the short line.
• Stand in the service box and hit the ball into the opposite back quarter of the court.

To Decrease Difficulty
• Stand closer to the front wall and use a shorter backswing.

2. Basic Serve Practice

Practice hitting basic serves on your own, from both the left and right service boxes. For this practice consider a successful serve one that hits the side wall at or behind the back of the service box.

 *Success Goal* =
8 out of 10 successful serves from right box ___
8 out of 10 successful serves from left box ___

✔ *Success Check*
• Prepare the racket before throwing the ball ___
• Take a small step before swinging ___
• Strike the ball as you would the forehand ___

3. Advanced Serve Practice

On your own, practice hitting advanced serves from the right service box. Remember to begin by facing the side wall nearer you with your back foot in the box. Work on the movement of turning your body to an open position and stepping across with your front foot toward the T as you strike the ball. Again, consider a successful serve one that hits the front wall and then the side wall at or behind the back of the service box.

 *Success Goal* = 8 out of 10 successful serves ___

✔ *Success Check*
• Begin facing side wall ___
• Step across toward T ___
• Face body to front wall when making contact ___

To Decrease Difficulty
• Begin with your body facing the front wall instead of the side wall.

4. Straight Volley Returns

Have a partner hit a high crosscourt from the front corner (see figure a). Hit a straight volley from the back and then hit a shot off the side wall back to your partner in the front corner (see figure b). Your partner should be aiming the crosscourts to hit high on the side wall close to the back of the service box as a good serve would. Your volleys should bounce behind the back of the service box, no farther from the side wall than the width of the service box.

Success Goal =

8 out of 10 forehand volleys bouncing behind the back of the service box ____

8 out of 10 backhand volleys bouncing behind the back of the service box ____

Success Check

• Stand facing the side wall ____
• Hit the ball between your body and the side wall ____
• Hit high on the front wall ____

To Increase Difficulty

• Have player B vary the pace and height of the crosscourts.

To Decrease Difficulty

• Have player B hit soft crosscourt shots that you can volley before the ball hits the side wall.

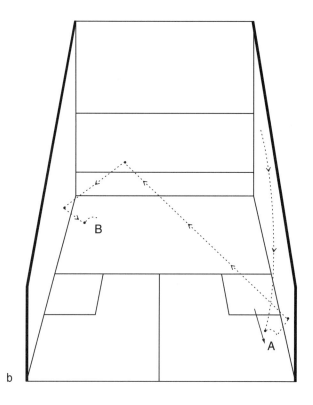

5. Crosscourt Volley Returns

With a partner, stand on opposite sides of the court at the back of the service boxes. Hit high crosscourt volleys to each other. Keep a rally going with your partner without the ball touching the floor.

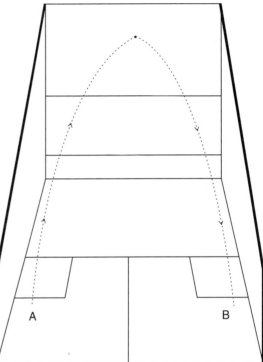

Success Goal = Rally 30 shots ___

Success Check
• Keep the wrist firm ___
• Punch through the ball ___
• Hit with plenty of width ___

To Increase Difficulty
• Keep the rally going without stepping in front of the back of the service box.

To Decrease Difficulty
• Let the ball bounce to keep the rally going.

6. Serve and Rally Game

Player A serves, and player B returns the serve with a straight volley or drive (see figure a). Then the two of you play a rally, hitting only straight drives (see figure b). Practice this with your partner first; then play a conditioned game in which every shot must bounce past the short line, no farther than a service-box width from the side wall.

Success Goal = Winning 2 out of 3 games against your partner ___

Success Check
• Make the serve hit the side wall ___
• Volley the return of serve whenever possible ___
• Circle around each other when hitting straight drives ___

To Increase Difficulty
• Make the target area smaller; that is, every shot must bounce behind the back of the service box.

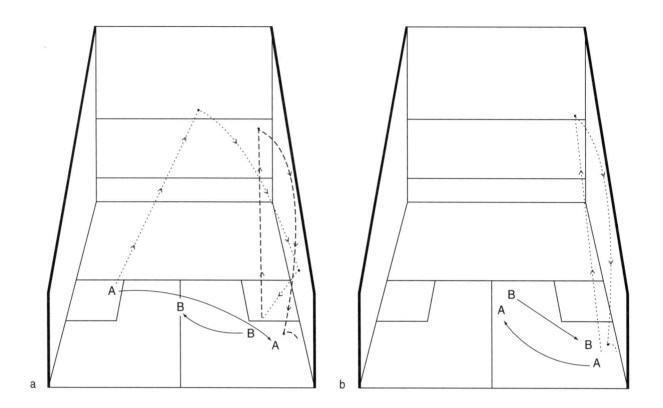

7. Serve and Crosscourt Rally Game

One player serves, and the other returns the serve with a crosscourt. Then rally crosscourt until one of you hits a shot that bounces outside the opposite back quarter of the court. Again, play this as a conditioned game with your partner.

Success Goal = Winning 2 out of 3 games against your partner ___

Success Check
• Volley whenever possible ___
• Prepare your racket early ___
• Hit high on the front wall ___

To Increase Difficulty
• Play a game in which you and your partner must volley. Any shot a player allows to bounce into the target area loses the point.

SERVE AND RETURN OF SERVE SUCCESS SUMMARY

You should begin by learning the basic serves from the right and left boxes. You can then consider mixing it up a bit with variations to keep your opponent guessing. Keeping in mind the basics of the forehand swing—racket up, wrist firm, and body still—will help on serves from both sides. To return a serve, you may either hit an attacking shot to the frontcourt, a defensive shot into the back corners, or a boast to the front corner. Volleying the serve will limit your opponent's preparation time, but if the serve is overhit you may want to let the ball bounce off the back wall. Try to hit the ball straight and be sure to allow yourself plenty of room to hit the ball, regardless of its position. Always be prepared with your racket up from the time your opponent begins the serve and always keep your eye on the ball. Have your coach critique your serve and return of serve using the Keys to Success checklists in figures 7.1, 7.3, and 7.5 through 7.8.

STEP 8

THE BOAST: HITTING OFF THE SIDE WALL

The walls of the court dramatically increase the variation of shots you can use in a squash match. They create the opportunity to hit angle shots off the side or back walls to the frontcourt, which allows you to escape some tricky situations in the back corners. In addition, you can attack your opponents with these angles, stretching them to the front corners.

A shot hit off one of the side walls or the back wall onto the front wall is called a *boast*. There are a variety of boasts. These include the trickle boast, skid boast, reverse angle, and back-wall boast, to name but a few.

Most top players use the boast sparingly at the beginning of the match, choosing instead to pin their opponent back with drives and volleys, and playing the boast only when necessary to hit the ball out of the back corners. As the game progresses, however, and their opponent becomes more tired, they begin to work their opponent to the front of the court. The boast, at this stage, becomes a potent offensive weapon.

Why Is the Boast Important?

The boast is a versatile shot. You can hit it from anywhere in the court and you can use it to attack, to defend, to deceive an unsuspecting opponent, or, as a last-resort shot, to keep you in the rally. For the novice player the boast is the easiest way to hit the ball to the front of the court. The drop shot requires developing good touch, which takes practice to master. The boast, on the other hand, is like hitting a drive into the side wall, and is therefore relatively easy once you can consistently hit a good drive.

As you start playing better players, you'll find that they'll begin to read your boasts more easily and will look to counterattack off them. This doesn't mean you should rule out the boast as an attacking shot, but it will require more disguise, and you should play

it only if you feel your opponent is not watching carefully enough or is out of position and will struggle to retrieve it.

The boast is most useful, however, as an easier way of hitting shots out of the back corners. When your opponent hits a drive to a good length, the ball is sometimes not going to bounce far enough away from the back wall for you to hit a drive. In these situations all you can do is hit the ball off the side wall (in extreme situations, the back wall) and onto the front wall.

How to Boast out of the Back Corners

When hitting the boast out of the back corners, use a midstance in the same way as you would for the drive. Your feet should be about shoulder-width apart, with your body turned farther toward the back wall than it would be for the drive (see figures 8.1a and 8.2a). Prepare your racket early and bend your knees because you'll be hitting the ball close to the floor.

Make sure that you don't set up too close to the back corner; give yourself enough room so that you don't hamper your swing. Make contact with the ball out by your front foot and hit the shot just as you would a drive into the side wall (see figures 8.1b and 8.2b).

As you follow through make sure that you keep your wrist firm and your racket face open. Abbreviate your follow-through slightly from your drive follow-through so that you get more of a punch at the end of the shot (see figures 8.1c and 8.2c).

Imagine another court next to yours and aim the ball toward the opposite front corner of that court. This will give you the correct angle to make the ball rebound off the side wall onto the front wall within a couple feet of the opposite side wall. Ideally, after hitting the front wall the ball should bounce close to the side-wall nick.

The most important aspect of this shot is to take your opponent away from the T and up to the front corner. So don't worry about whether the ball hits the floor or the side wall first after it has hit the front wall. Keep the ball as low as you can without risking hitting the tin; remember that the boast is a defensive shot intended to keep you in the rally, so don't be too ambitious! It isn't advisable to hit the shot too hard either, because this will cause a less accurate shot to bounce out into the middle of the court. Of-

ten, a softer shot will float nicely up into the front corner, giving you time to position yourself on the T for your opponent's return.

If the ball is close not only to the back wall but also to the side wall, you should use a short backswing and just try to jam the ball out off the side wall. Use hardly any follow-through because if you do you're likely to double-hit the ball (hit the ball a second time as it rebounds off the side wall). Keep the racket face open to make sure the ball goes upward to increase its chances of reaching the front wall.

FIGURE 8.1

KEYS TO SUCCESS

FOREHAND BOAST OUT OF THE BACK CORNER

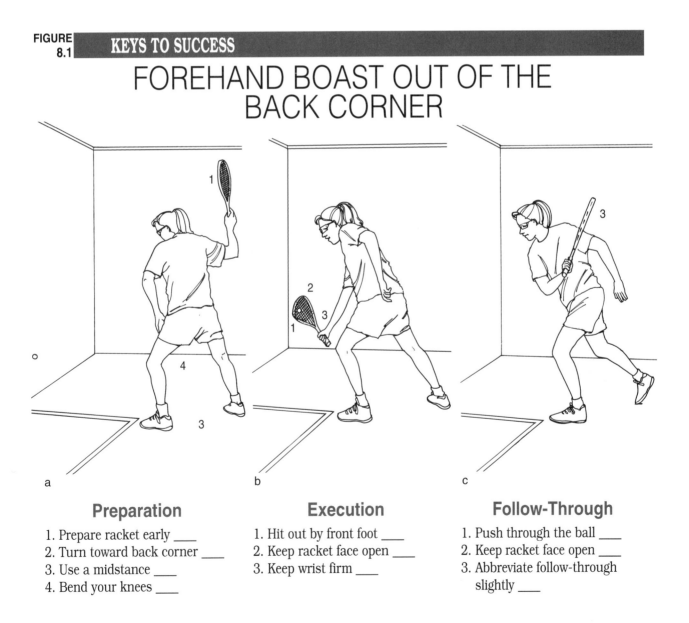

Preparation
1. Prepare racket early ___
2. Turn toward back corner ___
3. Use a midstance ___
4. Bend your knees ___

Execution
1. Hit out by front foot ___
2. Keep racket face open ___
3. Keep wrist firm ___

Follow-Through
1. Push through the ball ___
2. Keep racket face open ___
3. Abbreviate follow-through slightly ___

FIGURE 8.2

KEYS TO SUCCESS

BACKHAND BOAST OUT OF THE BACK CORNER

Preparation

1. Prepare racket early ___
2. Turn toward back corner ___
3. Use a midstance ___
4. Bend your knees ___

a

b

Execution

1. Hit out by front foot ___
2. Keep racket face open ___
3. Keep wrist firm ___

Follow-Through

1. Push through the ball ___
2. Keep racket face open ___
3. Abbreviate follow-through slightly ___

c

How to Boast From the Middle of the Court

This is often a reflex shot played when cutting off a drive and is usually played on the volley. You should aim this shot to come off the side wall and hit low in the middle of the front wall so that its second bounce on the floor is close to the side wall.

Early preparation is again the key to this shot (see figure 8.3a). You should also keep your wrist firm and punch through the ball (see figure 8.3b). The shot often requires only a short swing and not much pace on the ball. This is particularly true if your opponent hit a hard shot; it's then almost a block. If your opponent's shot was softer, punch through a little more quickly to reduce the time your opponent has to get to the front of the court to retrieve the shot. Always concentrate on keeping your swing controlled; in particular, avoid rolling over the wrist as you strike the ball, which may cause it to go into the tin.

FIGURE 8.3 **KEYS TO SUCCESS**

BOAST FROM THE MIDDLE OF THE COURT

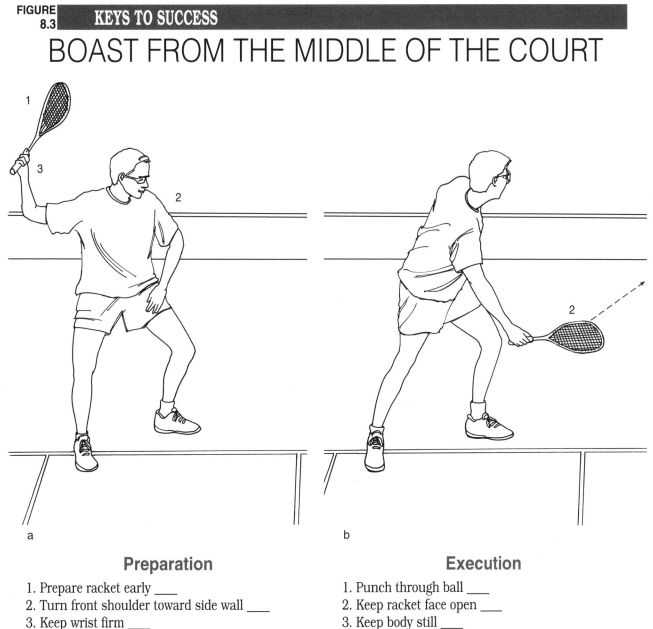

a

b

Preparation

1. Prepare racket early ___
2. Turn front shoulder toward side wall ___
3. Keep wrist firm ___

Execution

1. Punch through ball ___
2. Keep racket face open ___
3. Keep body still ___
4. Use a short swing ___

How to Boast From the Front of the Court

You play this shot, normally referred to as a trickle boast, from one of the front corners of the court. Try to make sure you hit this shot with plenty of disguise. Position yourself and shape up with a big backswing as if you were going to hit a hard drive (see figure 8.4a). Then, as you bring the racket face down to make contact with the ball, keep your wrist forward instead of pushing your racket face through (see figure 8.4b). Leading with your wrist in this manner will keep the racket face facing toward the side wall as you contact the ball. Swing through quite fast but with a shorter follow-through and slice the ball into the side wall. Keep the ball low to minimize your opponent's chances of retrieving the shot. If the large backswing is believable your opponent will be on his or her heels and won't be able to get to the front of the court fast enough to hit the ball before the second bounce. Beware, however, because if your opponent does reach the ball he or she will have the whole court to hit into, and you'll be stranded in the front corner. For this reason a drop shot (see step 9) is normally a better attacking shot to play from the front of the court. Only occasionally throw in the trickle boast. Yet, for the lower-level player who hasn't developed good touch with the drop, the trickle boast can be the most effective shot at the front of the court.

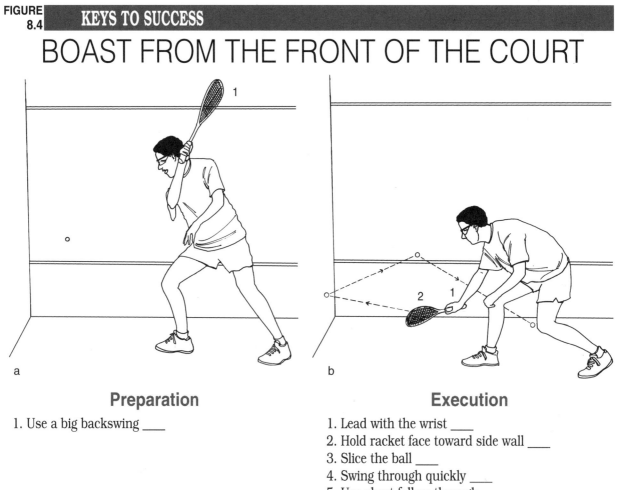

FIGURE 8.4

KEYS TO SUCCESS

BOAST FROM THE FRONT OF THE COURT

a

b

Preparation

1. Use a big backswing ___

Execution

1. Lead with the wrist ___
2. Hold racket face toward side wall ___
3. Slice the ball ___
4. Swing through quickly ___
5. Use short follow-through ___

Back-Wall Boast

This shot is a last-resort shot played when your opponent has hit a shot past you and there is no way you can hit a boast off the side wall. This is normally the case if you are at full stretch reaching behind you for the ball or if your opponent's shot came off the side wall and stayed so close to the back wall that you couldn't hit a boast far enough along the side wall to reach the front wall (see figure 8.5a).

When at full stretch for this shot, just concentrate on getting your racket face underneath the ball. Lift it so that after hitting the back wall, it travels high in the air and then drops onto the front wall (see figure 8.5b). Hit the shot just hard enough to guarantee that the ball will reach the front wall. The less pace you use, the more time you'll give yourself to get position on the T to cover your opponent's next shot. It's best to angle the shot so that after hitting the back wall it travels diagonally across the court to-

ward the opposite front corner. This reduces considerably the likelihood that you'll hit the ball out of court on the side wall. It also increases the chances that the ball will hit the front wall and then hug the side wall, making it difficult for your opponent to hit an attacking shot.

If you're hitting a back-wall boast because the ball is tight against the back wall, use a short, punchy backswing with virtually no follow-through. Make sure your racket face is open and try to jam the ball upward. This difficult shot requires much practice, but it's surprising how often, from a seemingly impossible position, you'll be able to get the ball back into play.

Remember that this shot should be your last option. Don't always rely on it to get the ball back into play. Against a good player you'll be setting up your opponent with an excellent opportunity to hit a winning shot or make you work hard to retrieve the next shot.

FIGURE 8.5

KEYS TO SUCCESS

BACK-WALL BOAST

Preparation

1. Face the back wall ___
2. Take a large step toward back wall ___
3. Bend down low ___

Execution

1. Place racket face underneath ball ___
2. Use a short swing ___
3. Hit soft looping shot to front wall ___

Reverse Angle

The reverse angle is a shot hit off the side wall farther from you and onto the front wall. To maintain the element of surprise, attempt the shot only occasionally. If your opponent reads the shot he or she may be able to get to the front of the court quickly and gain the initiative. This attacking shot is often most effective when hit from deep in the court with your opponent to your side. One of the best times to play this shot is when your opponent has overhit a shot and the ball has bounced far from the back wall. Make it look as if you're going to hit a crosscourt; prepare the racket early and wait for the ball to come in front of you before swinging (see figure 8.6a). The longer you can wait before hitting the ball, the more likely it is that your opponent will be back on his or her heels for the crosscourt. Then whip the ball across the court in front of your opponent. The ball should hit the side wall so that it comes back across the court to the opposite front corner after hitting the front wall (see figure 8.6b).

You can also play this shot when you're in front of your opponent. Be careful when using it from far up the court because if you hit it too high, your opponent will have a good opportunity to get to the ball and drive it past you to the back of the court. Normally, a straight or crosscourt drop is preferable to a reverse angle from the front of the court.

FIGURE 8.6 **KEYS TO SUCCESS**

REVERSE ANGLE

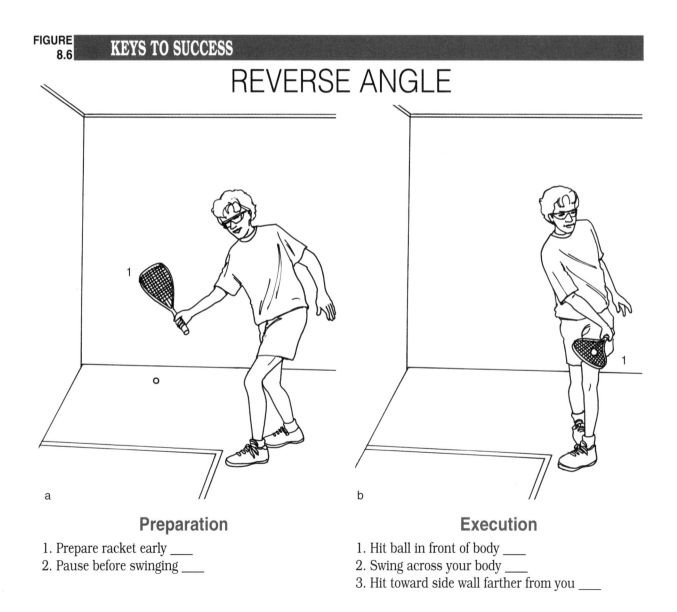

a

b

Preparation

1. Prepare racket early ___
2. Pause before swinging ___

Execution

1. Hit ball in front of body ___
2. Swing across your body ___
3. Hit toward side wall farther from you ___

Skid Boast

This is the only type of boast that doesn't end up in the frontcourt. Instead, you send the ball to the opposite back corner via the side wall nearer you (see figure 8.7a). To do this you must aim the ball higher on the side wall and closer to the front wall (see figure 8.7b). The ball should hit high in the center of the front wall and should then float to the opposite back corner (see figure 8.8). Use a more open racket face to get the necessary height on the shot. Use the shot sparingly because it is most effective if you can make your opponent move forward expecting a regular boast. This is a difficult shot to play; you risk giving your opponent an easy opportunity to hit a winner if you don't get the necessary height on the shot. So attempt this shot only when you are well balanced and not under pressure.

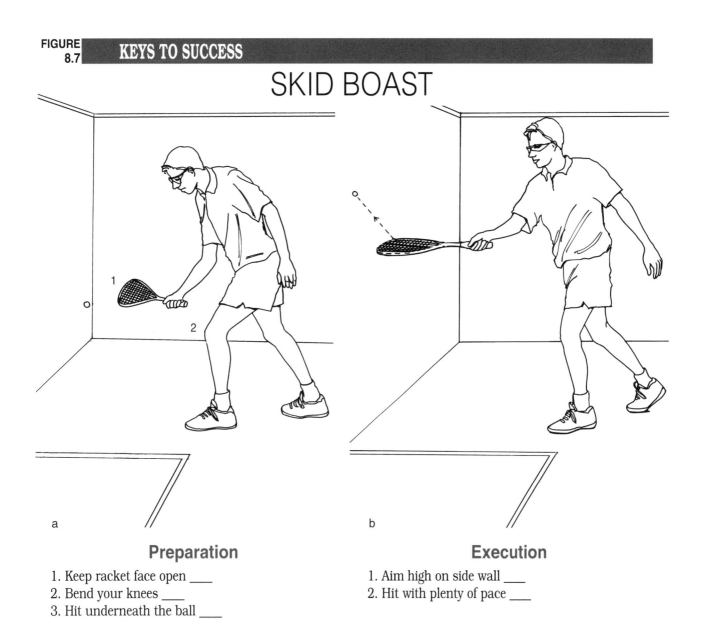

FIGURE 8.7   **KEYS TO SUCCESS**

SKID BOAST

a

b

Preparation

1. Keep racket face open ___
2. Bend your knees ___
3. Hit underneath the ball ___

Execution

1. Aim high on side wall ___
2. Hit with plenty of pace ___

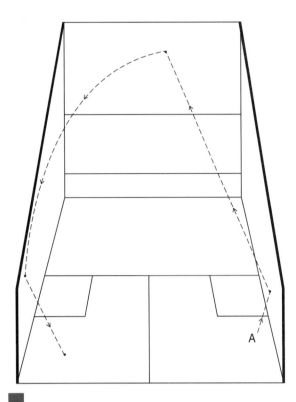

Figure 8.8 Ball path for the skid boast.

The skid boast is also more effective when played on a warmer court. This is because the ball will be bouncier, so it is easier to get the necessary power and height for the ball to reach the back of the court. On a cold court, the ball is unlikely to rebound far from the front wall, so your opponent will probably be able to volley the ball before it reaches the back court.

BOAST SUCCESS STOPPERS

Boasting the ball involves a fair amount of risk. A poorly hit boast will often end up in the tin or in a good position for your opponent. The following list of common errors and suggested corrections should help you to hit good boasts consistently.

Error	Correction
1. Ball doesn't reach the front wall.	1. Don't hit the ball from quite as far behind you and aim your shot farther along the side wall (closer to the front wall).
2. Ball bounces into the middle of the court.	2. Hit the ball with less power and don't aim the shot as far along the side wall.
3. Ball hits the tin.	3. Keep your racket face open so that you strike under the ball. Aim higher on the side wall, particularly from defensive positions.
4. Opponent hits winners off your boasts.	4. Use the shot less frequently so that you increase the element of surprise. When you must boast, hit with less power so that you have more time to recover to the T.

BOAST

DRILLS

1. Boast From Hand Feed

Stand near the back of the service box, about six feet from the side wall. Throw the ball against the side wall and, after it bounces (see figure a), hit a boast into the side wall (see figure b) so that it rebounds toward the opposite front corner. Try to hit your boast onto the front wall between the cut line and the tin.

Success Goal =

8 out of 10 forehand boasts hitting the front wall ___

8 out of 10 backhand boasts hitting the front wall ___

Success Check

• Turn slightly toward the back corner ___
• Use a midstance ___
• Bend your knees ___

To Increase Difficulty

• Throw the ball against the back wall instead of the side wall.
• Aim at a target on the floor, close to the side wall and about three feet from the front wall.

To Decrease Difficulty

• Move farther forward in the court.
• Concentrate only on hitting the ball above the tin.

a

b

2. Boast From Racket Feed

Stand in the back corner. Hit a straight drive back to yourself and then hit a boast off your drive. If possible you should hit your drive deep enough that it rebounds off the back wall after hitting the floor. Aim to make the boast bounce on a target about three feet from the front wall against the side wall.

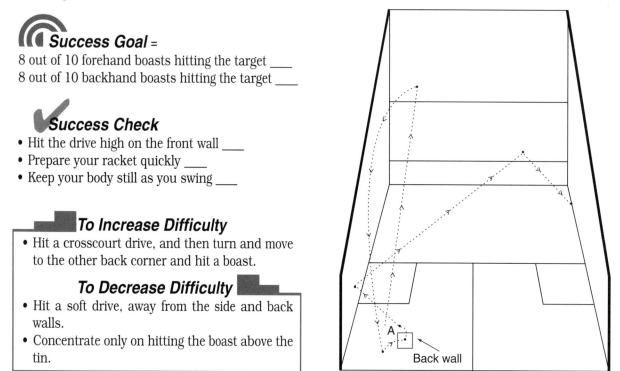

Back wall

Success Goal =
8 out of 10 forehand boasts hitting the target ____
8 out of 10 backhand boasts hitting the target ____

Success Check
• Hit the drive high on the front wall ____
• Prepare your racket quickly ____
• Keep your body still as you swing ____

To Increase Difficulty
• Hit a crosscourt drive, and then turn and move to the other back corner and hit a boast.

To Decrease Difficulty
• Hit a soft drive, away from the side and back walls.
• Concentrate only on hitting the boast above the tin.

3. Crosscourt Drive-Boast Routine

Have a partner stand in the front corner and hit crosscourt drives to you in the opposite back corner. After hitting the front wall, the crosscourts should preferably hit the side wall, then the floor, and then the back wall. From a position about two feet behind the T, move back, turn your body toward the back corner, and hit a boast back to your partner. Aim to hit the front wall between the cut line and the tin. After your shot, return to the position just behind the T for the next crosscourt.

Success Goal =
Hit 20 consecutive forehand boasts above the tin ____
Hit 20 consecutive backhand boasts above the tin ____

**Success Check**
- Give yourself plenty of room ___
- Turn your body toward the back corner ___
- Keep your wrist firm ___

To Decrease Difficulty
- Have your partner hit soft, high crosscourts that bounce into the middle of the court.
- Concentrate only on hitting above the tin.

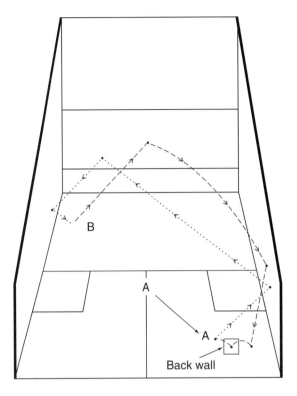

4. Drive and Boast

Put an object on the half-court line about five feet behind the T. Have a partner stand in the frontcourt and hit alternate forehand and backhand straight drives. Stand in the backcourt and hit alternate forehand and backhand boasts. After each boast you must move forward, around the object, and then back to the corner for the next boast.

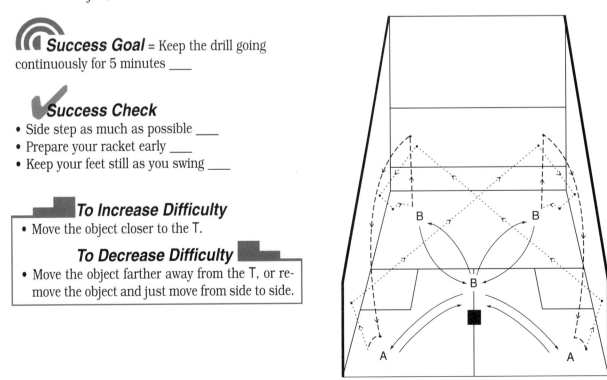

Success Goal = Keep the drill going continuously for 5 minutes ___

Success Check
- Side step as much as possible ___
- Prepare your racket early ___
- Keep your feet still as you swing ___

To Increase Difficulty
- Move the object closer to the T.

To Decrease Difficulty
- Move the object farther away from the T, or remove the object and just move from side to side.

5. Drive and Volley Boast

This drill is similar to drill 4, except you remove the object from the floor, stand farther forward in the court (about two feet behind the short line), and volley boast your partner's straight drives.

 *Success Goal* = Keep the drill going continuously for 3 minutes ___

 **To Increase Difficulty**
• Have your partner hit hard, low drives.

 *Success Check*
• Keep your wrist firm ___
• Use a short, punchy swing ___
• Side step across the court ___

6. Random Boasts

Have a partner stand in the front corner and hit either straight or crosscourt drives to the back corners. You must stand in the backcourt, move into position, and hit boasts from out of the back corners.

Success Goal = Keep the drill going continuously for 5 minutes ___

To Increase Difficulty
• Allow your partner to hit to any area of the court, while you must hit a boast.

To Decrease Difficulty
• Have your partner alternately hit straight and crosscourt drives.

Success Check
• Don't rush at the ball ___
• Carefully watch your opponent strike the ball ___

7. Drive-Drive-Boast

Stand on the T with a partner standing in the back corner. Hit a straight drive to your partner. Your partner hits a straight drive, and you move into the back corner and hit a boast. Your partner then moves up to the opposite front corner to hit a straight drive. You then hit another straight drive, and your partner moves to the back corner to boast. Keep your movement smooth and try to move through the T. Particularly when moving from the back corner to the opposite front corner, you should avoid moving across to the side wall too much because this will lead you to approach the ball from behind rather than from the side.

 *Success Goal* = Keep the drill going continuously for 5 minutes ___

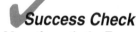 *Success Check*
• Move through the T ___
• Volley whenever possible ___
• Keep your movement smooth ___

8. Back Boast, Front Boast

Have a partner stand in the front corner and hit a straight drive. You hit a boast from the back corner. Your partner then hits a straight drop. You must run diagonally across the court to hit a trickle boast from the front. Your partner then drives to the back corner again. You run diagonally to the back corner and boast. When moving back from the front corner run backward to the T, then turn and move into position for the ball in the backcourt.

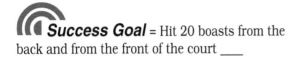 **Success Goal** = Hit 20 boasts from the back and from the front of the court ____

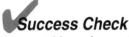 **Success Check**
• Move quickly and smoothly ____
• Prepare your racket early ____
• Run backward from the front ____

To Increase Difficulty
• Have your partner hit lower drops and hard-hit, low drives.

To Decrease Difficulty
• Have your partner hit high drop shots to give you plenty of time to move to the front.

9. Crosscourt-Boast Rally

Player A stands in the front corner, player B on the T, and player C in the opposite back corner. Player A hits a crosscourt and then turns and circles back toward the back corner, staying away from the middle of the court. Player C, in the back corner, hits a boast and then moves forward to the T. Player B moves forward to the front corner to hit a crosscourt off the boast. Once you get into the rhythm of this routine, you'll have no problem remembering which way to move and when it's your turn to hit. To begin with, however, it's easy to be confused and end up in the wrong position. Stay aware of where the ball and your partners are to avoid potentially hazardous situations.

Success Goal = Keep the drill going continuously for 5 minutes ____

Success Check
• Always watch the ball ____
• Don't rush ____
• Give yourself room to hit ____

To Decrease Difficulty
• Hit shots higher to allow more time to move into the correct positions to hit.

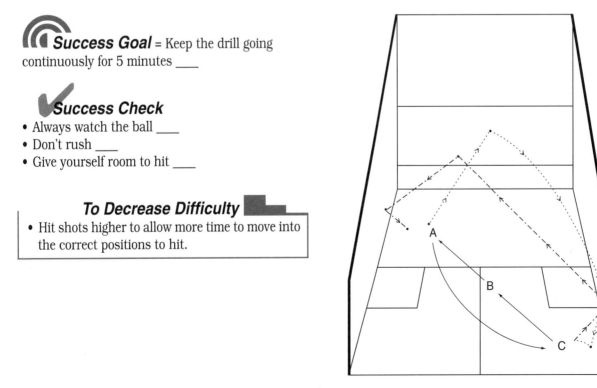

BOAST SUCCESS SUMMARY

As a beginner, you'll find the boast is the easiest way to move your opponent to the front of the court. As your game develops and you begin to play better players, you'll find that your opponents look to counterattack off your boast. The boast can still be part of your attacking arsenal, but you'll have to be more choosy about when to hit it and you'll need to hit it with more disguise. For all players, however, the boast will always be an important shot for working the ball out of the back corners. Often it's the only way that you can return an opponent's shot that is dying close to the back wall. Different types of boasts—the trickle boast, skid boast, back-wall boast, and reverse angle—are hit from different positions on the court. By learning them all you'll add variety to your game and become a much tougher opponent. Focus at first, however, on the basic boast out of the back corners. Ask someone to critique your boast using the Keys to Success checklists in figures 8.1 through 8.7.

STEP 9

DROP AND LOB SHOTS: MOVING YOUR OPPONENT WHERE YOU WANT

One of the most frustrating experiences for a young, fit, aspiring squash player is to come unstuck against an old, overweight player who maneuvers the younger opponent to all corners of the court using deft drops and high lobs. The drop and lob shots complement each other perfectly because they require similar swings, are hit from similar positions, yet end up in opposite areas of the court. For this reason, this step introduces both shots at the same time. Compare the similarities between the shots and see how they can be used together to negate completely the game of a harder hitting, quicker opponent.

A drop shot is an attacking shot that you hit softy just above the tin on the front wall so that it dies in the frontcourt. You can play it from any position in the court, although the deeper you are, the greater the chance of making an error. Well-executed drop shots often win rallies outright, although your goal should only be to stretch your opponent forward to the front of the court.

The lob shot is generally a defensive shot you use when you're stretched at the front of the court. The object of the shot is to hit a high, soft shot over the head of your opponent that drops into the back corner. Hitting the ball high not only gives your opponent a difficult return, either with a high volley or a shot out of the back corner, but also gives you time to recover into position. You can also use the lob to slow the pace of the game. This is a good tactic to use if you're losing and need to disrupt your opponent's rhythm. You can also use the lob as an attacking shot. When you have time at the front of the court, set up as if you're going to play a drop. This will draw your opponent forward, and you can then lob the ball over your incoming opponent's head.

Why Is the Drop Shot Important?

At the top level the drop shot is the main weapon used to win rallies. Use the drop either as the winning shot after you've forced your opponent to hit a weak shot, or as a way to move your opponent out of position so that you can hit a winner to the open court with the next shot. The advantage of the shot is that it forces your opponent to hurry into the front corner with little time to play a good shot. Even though a drop shot will often turn out to be a winning shot, you should think of it as a way of working your opponent, always expecting your opponent to retrieve the ball.

The drop shot is particularly effective if you can move quickly to the front of the court following an opponent's boast from the back of the court. This will force your opponent to run diagonally across the court. Experienced players learn to read their opponent's boast shot so they can pounce on it at the front of the court with a delicate drop.

How to Perform the Drop Shot

The drop shot is played like a slow drive, with slightly less backswing and very little follow-through. As you prepare for the shot, bend low to help control the racket face as you strike the ball. Lift the racket face up enough on the backswing to make it look as if you are about to hit a drive. Step across on your front foot (see figures 9.1a and 9.2a).

Make sure that you have the racket face open as you strike the ball so that you slice the shot (see

KEYS TO SUCCESS

FOREHAND DROP SHOT

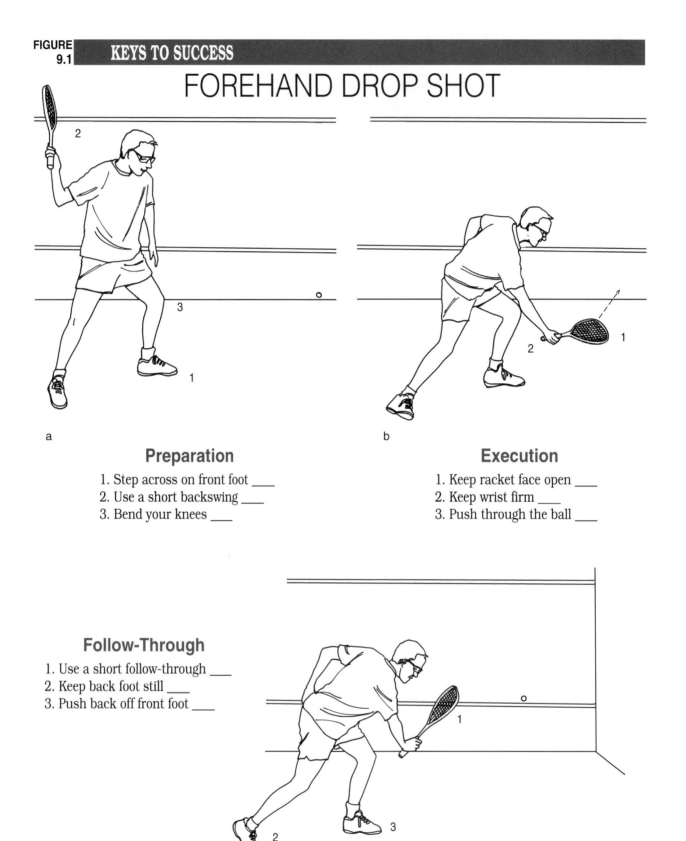

a

b

Preparation

1. Step across on front foot ___
2. Use a short backswing ___
3. Bend your knees ___

Execution

1. Keep racket face open ___
2. Keep wrist firm ___
3. Push through the ball ___

Follow-Through

1. Use a short follow-through ___
2. Keep back foot still ___
3. Push back off front foot ___

c

FIGURE
9.2 **KEYS TO SUCCESS**

BACKHAND DROP SHOT

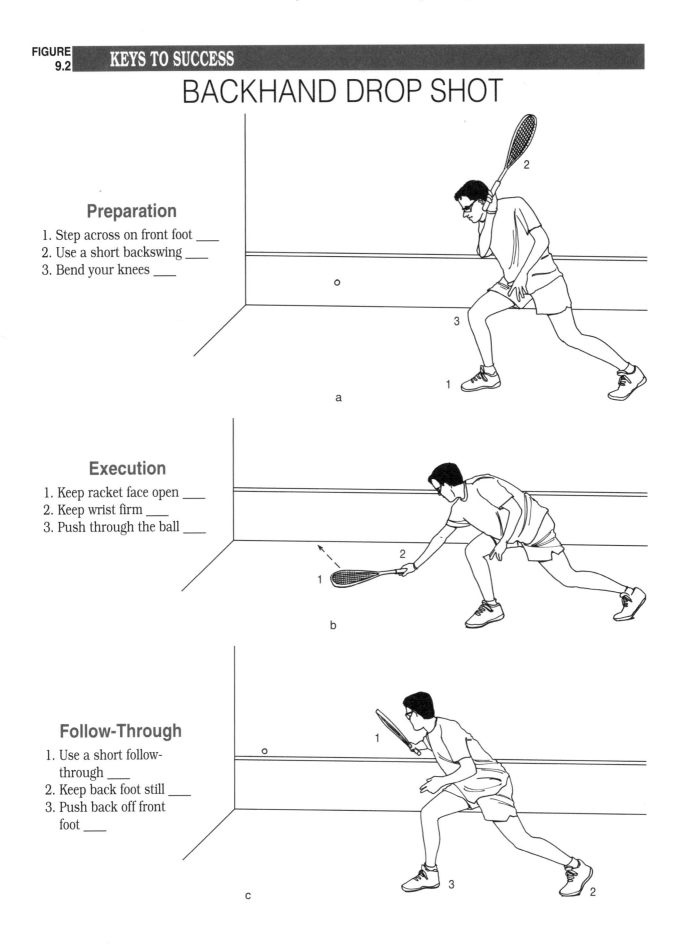

Preparation

1. Step across on front foot ___
2. Use a short backswing ___
3. Bend your knees ___

a

Execution

1. Keep racket face open ___
2. Keep wrist firm ___
3. Push through the ball ___

b

Follow-Through

1. Use a short follow-through ___
2. Keep back foot still ___
3. Push back off front foot ___

c

figures 9.1b and 9.2b). This will help the ball die after it has hit the front wall. Avoid using too much wrist to slice the ball because this often leads to mishitting the shot. It's best to keep the wrist firm and push through the ball on impact.

Limit your follow-through and try to push back off your front foot quickly so that you can recover to a position to cover your opponent's shot (see figures 9.1c and 9.2c). The timing of your step into the shot is important. Try to step and swing at almost the same time so that you can get your momentum into the shot.

Always keep in mind that the drop shot is a way of working your opponent to the front of the court. You shouldn't hit this shot so high that you set up your opponent for a winner, or so low that you risk hitting the tin. Also, if you can angle the shot toward the nick or if you can keep the ball close to the side wall, you'll add to your opponent's difficulties.

Why Is the Lob Shot Important?

Use the lob shot primarily as a defensive shot. Normally, when your opponent's good shot has forced you to full stretch at the front of the court, the lob is the only shot that will keep you in the rally. A straight drive is usually impossible because the ball is so far in front of you. Your opponent will be on the T, just waiting for a crosscourt drive to hit to the opposite back corner to make you run the diagonal. A drop is a possibility but may be difficult to execute well enough to avoid leaving you stranded at the front of the court. The alternative is to lift the ball as high as you can in the hope that it will go over your opponent's head. This will force your opponent to move to the back corner to retrieve it or at least stretch up and hit a difficult high volley. A well-executed lob can often immediately turn a defensive position into an offensive one.

How to Perform the Lob Shot

As with the drop shot, it's important to bend down to the ball for the lob shot. Stretch forward with your front foot, prepare the racket face early, but use a shorter backswing than you use for the drive (see figures 9.3a and 9.4a).

Get the racket face underneath the ball as you strike it so that you can lift it high onto the front wall (see figures 9.3b and 9.4b). A slight flick with the wrist will sometimes provide the lift you need on the shot, but be careful not to use so much wrist that you lose control of the shot.

As you follow through keep your body still and finish with the racket face up high (see figures 9.3c and 9.4c). Once you have finished the shot push back off the front foot and move back to the middle of the court.

The lob can be hit either straight or crosscourt. Crosscourt lobs are normally easier to hit, particularly if you're stretching forward for the shot. You also have more room for error on a crosscourt lob. If you hit straight, the ball must stay close to the side wall or you may risk giving up a penalty point by hitting it back to yourself. Aim the crosscourt lob to hit the side wall close to the back of the service box so that it bounces close to the back wall. Be careful about hitting out of court. It's better to hit high on the front wall and down the middle of the court than risk hitting out of court on the side wall or not getting the ball over your opponent's head.

FIGURE
9.3 **KEYS TO SUCCESS**

FOREHAND LOB SHOT

Preparation

1. Stretch forward with front foot ___
2. Use a short backswing ___
3. Bend low ___

a

b

Execution

1. Place racket face underneath ball ___
2. Flick the wrist slightly ___
3. Aim high on front wall ___

c

Follow-Through

1. Keep body still ___
2. Finish with racket high ___
3. Push back off front foot ___

FIGURE 9.4

BACKHAND LOB SHOT

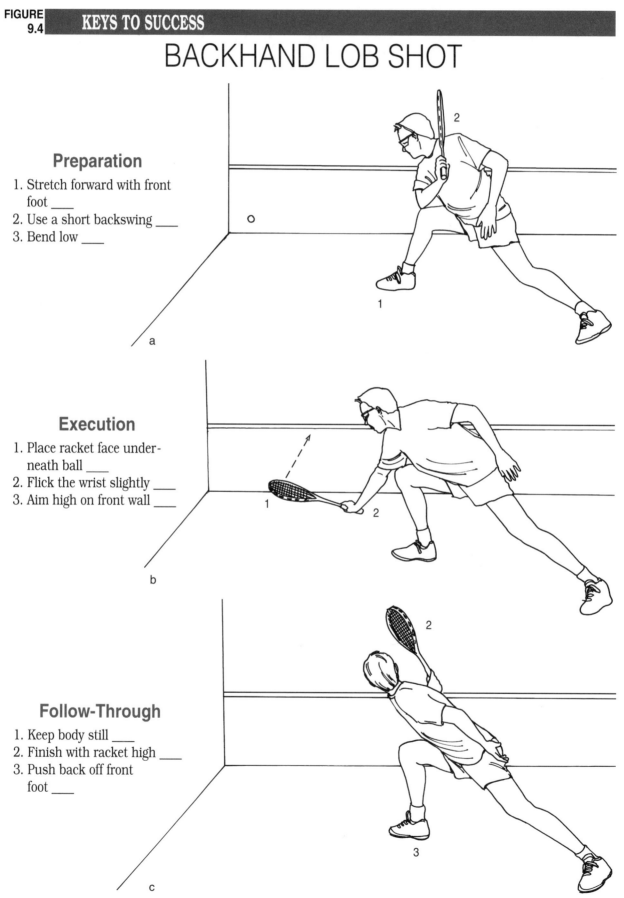

Preparation

1. Stretch forward with front foot ___
2. Use a short backswing ___
3. Bend low ___

a

Execution

1. Place racket face underneath ball ___
2. Flick the wrist slightly ___
3. Aim high on front wall ___

b

Follow-Through

1. Keep body still ___
2. Finish with racket high ___
3. Push back off front foot ___

c

DROP AND LOB SHOT SUCCESS STOPPERS

You'll know if you're hitting poor drop or lob shots because you'll be continually setting up your opponent with easy attacking opportunities. If you're forcing your opponent to hit from a stretched position, either stretched forward or stretched high, then you're hitting reasonably successful drops and lobs.

Error	Correction
Drop Shot	
1. Drop shots hit tin.	1. Keep the racket face open and push through the ball. Aim higher on the front wall to give yourself more room for error.
2. Drop shots hit too hard or too high on the front wall.	2. Keep your wrist firm and use a shorter swing. Don't follow through too much.
3. Drop shots hit side wall before front wall.	3. Keep your wrist firm, give yourself plenty of room to swing, and make sure you hit the ball approximately level with your front foot.
4. Drop shot lacks control.	4. Attempt a drop only when you have time to set up for the shot. Make sure that you keep your body still as you swing.
Lob Shot	
1. Not enough height on your lobs.	1. Bend lower to get underneath the ball. Flick your wrist slightly to lift the ball more.
2. Ball goes out of court.	2. Keep your wrist a little firmer as you swing. Don't aim as far across the front wall when hitting a crosscourt lob.
3. Lobs lack control.	3. Keep your body and feet still as you swing through.

DROP AND LOB SHOTS

DRILLS

1. Hand Feed for Drop

Stand about 10 feet from the front wall. Throw the ball against the side wall and after it bounces hit a straight drop. Aim your shot just above the tin and close to the side wall. Place a target on the floor about three feet from the front wall and against the side wall. Try to make your shots bounce on the target.

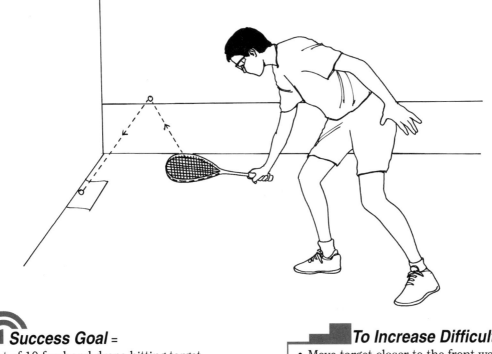

Success Goal =

8 out of 10 forehand drops hitting target ____
8 out of 10 backhand drops hitting target ____

Success Check

• Step and swing almost simultaneously ____
• Keep wrist firm ____
• Keep racket face open ____

To Increase Difficulty

• Move target closer to the front wall.
• Stand farther from front wall.
• Throw the ball against the front wall, run forward, and hit drop shot.

To Decrease Difficulty

• Make target larger.

2. Hand Feed for Lob

Stand in the middle of the court about 10 feet from the front wall. Throw the ball into the front corner so it hits the front wall and then the side wall. Run forward and hit a straight lob into the back corner. Step forward with your front foot and bend low so that you can get your racket face underneath the ball. Lift the ball high onto the front wall so that the ball arcs into the back corner. Aim for the ball to bounce between the back of the service box and the back wall no farther from the side wall than the width of the service box.

 **Success Goal** =

8 out of 10 forehand lobs bouncing behind service box ___

8 out of 10 backhand lobs bouncing behind service box ___

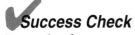 **Success Check**

• Keep racket face open ___
• Bend low ___
• Aim high on front wall ___

To Increase Difficulty

• Aim for a target on the floor about three feet from the back wall, against the side wall.
• Hit crosscourt lobs toward the opposite back corner instead of straight lobs.

To Decrease Difficulty

• Stand about six feet from the side wall, throw the ball against the side wall, and then step across and hit either straight or crosscourt lobs.

3. Racket Feed for Drop

Stand on the T. Feed the ball across your body so that it hits the front wall and then the side wall. Turn your body and hit a straight drop. Think about angling your shot so that the ball hits the front wall and then hits the floor close to the side-wall nick. Set a target on the floor against the side wall, three feet from the front wall.

 **Success Goal** =

8 out of 10 forehand drops hitting the target ___
8 out of 10 backhand drops hitting the target ___

Success Check

• Step across with front foot ___
• Use a short backswing ___
• Slice the ball ___

To Increase Difficulty

• Hit crosscourt drops instead of straight drops.
• Feed a high boast and then run forward to hit a straight drop.

To Decrease Difficulty

• Make target larger.

4. Racket Feed for Lob

Stand on the T, feed a high boast, and then run forward and hit alternating straight and crosscourt lobs into the back corners. Put targets in the back corners. For the straight lob the target should be about three feet from the back wall and against the side wall. For the crosscourt lob the target should also be about three feet from the back wall but slightly away from the side wall. Your goal on the crosscourt lob will be to make the ball hit the side wall and bounce onto the target.

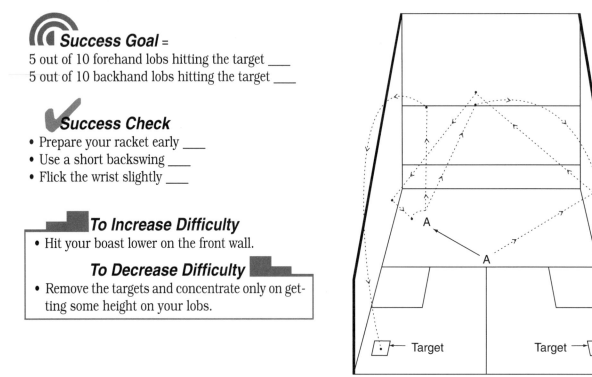

 Success Goal =

5 out of 10 forehand lobs hitting the target ___
5 out of 10 backhand lobs hitting the target ___

✔ Success Check

- Prepare your racket early ___
- Use a short backswing ___
- Flick the wrist slightly ___

To Increase Difficulty

- Hit your boast lower on the front wall.

To Decrease Difficulty

- Remove the targets and concentrate only on getting some height on your lobs.

5. Backcourt Drops

Stand in the back corner and play an overhit drive that bounces off the back wall. Then hit a drop shot toward a target about five feet from the front wall against the side wall. Use a little more follow-through to make sure you hit the ball with enough power to reach the front wall above the tin. Give yourself some room for error on the front wall but keep the ball close to the side wall. You need plenty of slice to make the ball die quickly after hitting the front wall so make sure that your racket face is open.

 Success Goal =

8 out of 10 forehand drops hitting the target ___
8 out of 10 backhand drops hitting the target ___

✔ Success Check

- Aim higher on the front wall ___
- Slice the ball ___
- Use a little more follow-through ___

To Increase Difficulty
- Move the target closer to the front wall.
- Vary the pace of your drop shots.
- Attempt crosscourt drops instead of straight drop shots.
- Play overhit crosscourt drives; then turn your body and hit a straight drop on the opposite side.

To Decrease Difficulty
- Make the target larger.
- Move the target farther from the front wall.
- Hit your overhit drives farther from the side wall.

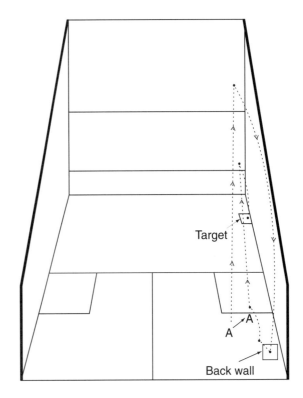

Target

Back wall

6. Drop From a Partner's Feed

Have a partner stand in the frontcourt about six feet from both the front wall and the side wall. Have your partner feed a straight shot that bounces about halfway between the front wall and the short line. You move forward from the T, hit a straight drop, and then push back to the T. Mark a line on the floor about three feet from the front wall. Try to hit all your drop shots so that they bounce in front of this line close to the side wall. Your partner should feed continuously rather than stop after each drop shot.

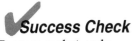 Success Goal =
8 out of 10 forehand drops bouncing in front of the line ___
8 out of 10 backhand drops bouncing in front of the line ___

✔ Success Check
- Prepare racket early ___
- Step across with front foot ___
- Bend your knees ___

To Increase Difficulty
- Have your partner alternately feed a shot that bounces between the front wall and the short line and a shot that bounces in the service box.
- Have your partner mix up the feeds to work you up and down the length of the court.

To Decrease Difficulty
- Mark the line farther from the front wall.
- Have your partner stop after each drop so that you have more time to prepare for the next feed.

7. Lob From Partner's Feed

Have a partner stand in the back corner and feed a short shot to the frontcourt. You move forward from the T, hit a straight lob, and then push back to the T. Again, as in drill 4, set a target at the back of the court.

Success Goal =

5 out of 10 forehand lobs bouncing on the target ___

5 out of 10 backhand lobs bouncing on the target ___

✔ Success Check

• Watch the ball ___
• Step across on your front foot ___
• Keep racket face underneath the ball ___

To Increase Difficulty

• Have your partner feed boasts for you to hit crosscourt lobs.

To Decrease Difficulty

• Make the target larger.
• Have your partner feed higher on the front wall.

8. Pressure Drops

Have a partner stand close to the side wall, about five feet from the front wall. Your partner should either hand feed or racket feed the ball so that it bounces about two feet from the front wall. You must move forward from the T, hit a drop, and then backpedal to the T. This drill should work you hard for a short period. Your partner's feeds should force you to move quickly and to stretch forward with your front foot to reach the ball before it bounces twice. You'll only need a very short swing—just enough to push the ball onto the front wall. Backpedal quickly after the shot and make sure you return behind the short line.

Success Goal =

12 out of 15 forehand drops hit above the tin ___
12 out of 15 backhand drops hit above the tin ___

✔ Success Check

• Stretch front foot forward ___
• Keep wrist firm ___
• Use a short push with racket face ___

To Decrease Difficulty

• Have your partner feed higher on the front wall to give you more time to get to the ball.

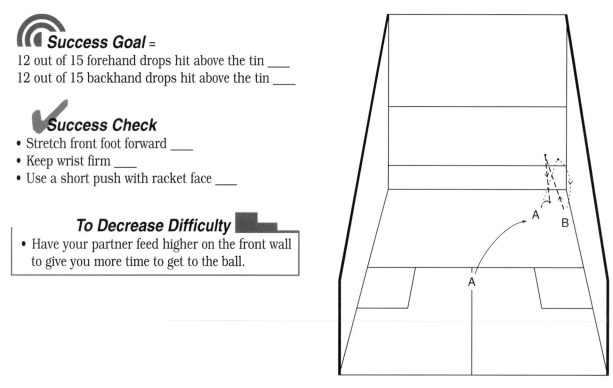

9. Drive Your Drops

This drill forces you to shorten your follow-through because if you don't, you won't have enough time to prepare the racket for the drive. Have a partner stand in the back corner and feed a straight shot to the frontcourt. From the T, move forward, hit a straight drop, and then hit a straight drive (back to your partner) off your drop shot. Aim to hit the drop shot low enough so that after the drop you can drag your back foot to your front foot. Then step forward again on the front foot for the drive.

 **Success Goal** =

8 out of 10 times successfully completing both the forehand drop and drive ____

8 out of 10 times successfully completing both the backhand drop and drive ____

✔ **Success Check**

• Prepare racket quickly ____
• Keep body still when driving ____
• Stay low ____

To Increase Difficulty

• Have your partner hit boasts; you go from side to side, hitting straight drops followed by straight drives.
• Have your partner hit a boast; you hit a cross-court drop and then move across to hit a straight drive.

10. Lob and Boast Routine

Have a partner stand in the backcourt and move from side to side, alternately hitting forehand and backhand boasts. You stand in the frontcourt moving from side to side, alternately hitting forehand and backhand straight lobs. Try to move to and from the T between shots. If you're getting enough height on your lobs you should be able to get back to the T in plenty of time for the next shot.

Success Goal = Keep drill going continuously for 5 minutes ____

✔ **Success Check**

• Move forward in slight J shape ____
• Prepare your racket early ____
• Keep your body still as you swing ____

To Increase Difficulty

• Have your partner hit straight drop shots for you to hit crosscourt lobs.
• Have your partner hit straight drop shots for you to alternate between hitting straight and crosscourt lobs.

To Decrease Difficulty

• Make the target larger.
• Have your partner hit the boasts higher on the front wall.

11. Boast and Drop Pressure Drill

Have a partner stand in the front corner and hit a crosscourt drive. You stand at the back of the court and hit a boast (see figure a). Your partner then hits a straight drop. You must run forward and hit a straight drop off the drop (see figure b). Your partner will then hit another crosscourt, taking you to the back of the court to boast again. As you move forward, think about moving through the T. Always move between your partner and the side wall. Once you have hit the drop, push backward to the T, again staying between your partner and the side wall. Then turn and move back for the boast.

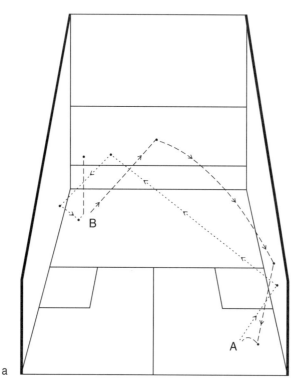
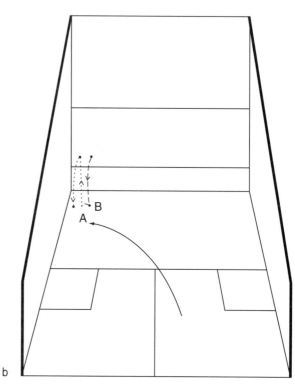

a   b

Success Goal =

12 out of 15 forehand drops above the tin ___
12 out of 15 backhand drops above the tin ___

✔ Success Check

• Step forward with front foot ___
• Prepare racket early ___
• Use a short follow-through ___

To Increase Difficulty

• Have your partner hit either straight or crosscourt drops; you must hit a straight drop to whichever front corner the ball goes to.
• Have your partner randomly hit straight drops and crosscourt drives; you hit boasts off the crosscourts, straight drops off the drops.

To Decrease Difficulty

• Have your partner hit higher drops to give you more time to get to the ball.

12. Boast-Drop-Drive

Your partner starts by hitting a boast from the back corner. You stand in the front corner and hit a straight drop. Your partner then runs forward and hits a straight drive off your drop. You must then run back and hit a boast, your partner straight drops, and you run forward and hit a straight drive. After hitting the drop move back to the middle, giving your partner room to move between you and the side wall. Also, remember to go through the T when moving forward after the boast.

 *Success Goal* = Keep drill going continuously for 5 minutes ___

 *Success Check*
- Move through the T ___
- Move quickly and smoothly ___
- Keep body still when swinging ___

 **To Increase Difficulty**
- Hit crosscourt drops instead of straight drops.
- Let the person hitting the drop choose to hit either straight or crosscourt.

To Decrease Difficulty
- Instead of keeping the drill going continuously, stop after you've each hit a boast, a drop, and a drive so that you can catch your breath, and then repeat.

13. Back Versus Front Lobs

Play a conditioned game in which your partner can hit any shot bouncing in front of the short line. You must hit either a straight or crosscourt lob. Play the game with point-per-rally scoring to 9, with you serving each time.

Success Goal = Win 2 out of 3 games against your opponent ___

Success Check
- Turn your head to watch the ball in the backcourt ___
- Move back to the T after each shot ___
- Keep your racket face open ___

To Increase Difficulty
- Play that you must hit either all straight lobs or all crosscourt lobs.

To Decrease Difficulty
- Play that your opponent must hit either all straight drops or all boasts.

14. Two Ball Feeds for Lob

Two feeders, each with a ball, stand in the back corners and hit short feeds to the front corners. You must move from side to side, alternately hitting forehand and backhand straight lobs. Try to watch the feeders as they strike the ball. Concentrate on stepping across on your front foot for each shot. Place a target on the floor in each back corner against the side wall and about three feet from the back wall. See how many times you can hit the targets.

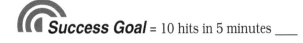 **Success Goal** = 10 hits in 5 minutes ___

 **Success Check**
• Watch the ball ___
• Bend low ___
• Side step across the court ___

To Increase Difficulty
• Have your feeders feed more quickly and lower on the front wall.

To Decrease Difficulty
• Make the targets larger.
• Have your feeders feed more slowly and higher on the front wall.

DROP AND LOB SHOT SUCCESS SUMMARY

If you want to win rallies you must learn the finer points of the drop. If you want to stay in rallies you must develop a good lob shot. The drop—a softly hit shot that hits the front wall and dies soon after—relies on a shortened backswing with some element of disguise. The lob—a soft shot hit high onto the front wall to arc into the back corner—is usually a defensive shot. Use it when you're under pressure to slow the game and move your opponent into the backcourt. Have an observer watch you practice your lobs and drops and rate them according to the Keys to Success checklists in figures 9.1 through 9.4.

STEP
10
KILL SHOTS: ATTACKING YOUR OPPONENT

Watching a player who can hit an array of kill shots on the squash court can be exhilarating. But it can be disheartening if you are the one facing that player. Such an opponent will dispatch the slightest wayward shot into the nick, leaving you chasing the ball as it rolls along the floor.

Kill shots are hit hard with slice, just above the tin and, if possible, angled toward the nick. Because the shot must be hit low on the front wall, there is little room for error. A shot hit too high will bounce up into the middle of the court, giving your opponent the advantage; a shot hit too low will hit the tin. Therefore, you should attempt a kill shot only when you have drawn a loose shot from your opponent and have the ball sitting up nicely for you. You should practice the kill shot before attempting it in match situations. You must feel confident about playing the kill shot or it will end up turning good opportunities into points lost.

Why Is the Kill Shot Important?

In a tight match the player who often comes out on top is the one prepared to step up and attack. You can do this, as discussed earlier, by volleying more. Another way of attacking your opponent, when left with the right opportunity, is attempting to kill the ball (hit it so it is unreturnable).

If you don't develop a kill shot, you'll often find yourself having difficulty finishing off a rally, even if your opponent is hitting loose shots. This is particularly true if you're playing on a hot court where the ball is bouncing up more than usual. In these conditions it can be difficult to put away your opponent with drops, good-length drives, and lobs. If you can't hit a kill shot you'll win only by wearing down your opponent, which can often take a great physical toll on you.

How to Perform the Straight Kill

You can play this shot from anywhere in the court as long as the ball isn't too close to the side or back walls. You should never attempt the shot if you feel at all rushed. Generally, the farther back in the court you are, the harder the shot is. Some players use the kill effectively off overhit shots that have bounced off the side and back toward the middle of the court.

As with all shots make sure you have the racket prepared early. Step across on your front foot, turning your front shoulder toward the side wall (see figures 10.1a and 10.2a). Have your racket face open and use a high backswing.

Strike the ball earlier than you do with the drive, that is, closer to the top of the bounce. As you swing, think about trying to hit down the back of the ball (see figures 10.1b and 10.2b). By using an open racket face you should be able to hit with plenty of slice. What you need to develop as you practice this shot is the right combination of racket-head speed and control. Your wrist and grip should be relaxed so that you can whip the racket face through with plenty of pace. You must not lose control of the racket face, however, or the open face will cause you to mis-hit the shot.

As you follow through begin to grip the racket more tightly (see figures 10.1c and 10.2c). This will enable you to control the swing right through the completion of the shot.

Aim the ball just above the tin and angle it toward the nick. Always attempt to hit the nick because this is what will make the shot unreturnable. Some players think that hitting the nick is just luck. This isn't true. The more you practice, the more you'll develop the feel for the sort of angle you need to hit the nick.

FIGURE 10.1 **KEYS TO SUCCESS**

FOREHAND STRAIGHT KILL SHOT

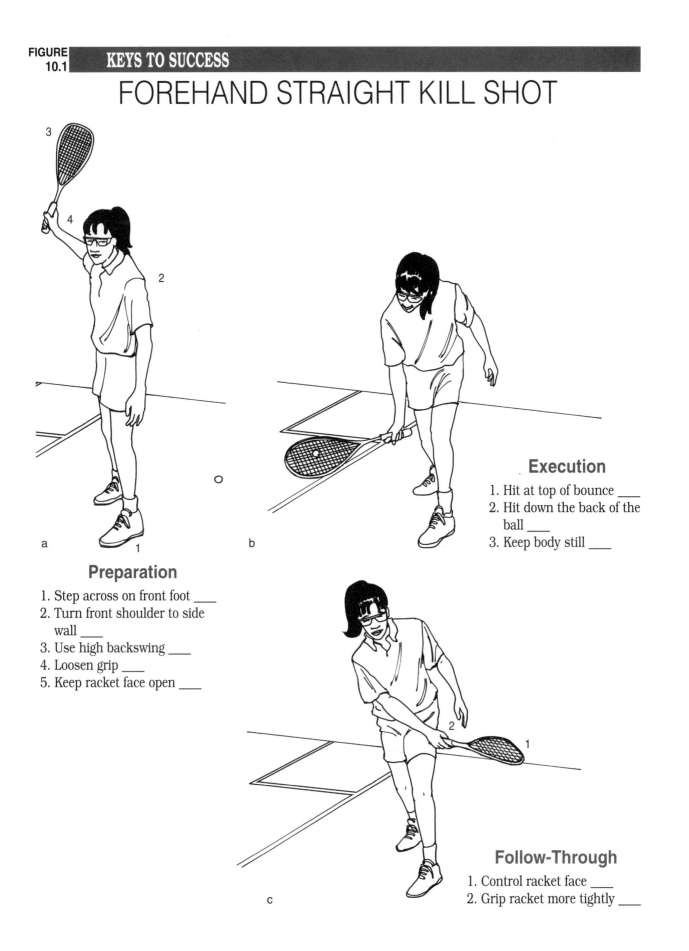

Preparation

1. Step across on front foot ___
2. Turn front shoulder to side wall ___
3. Use high backswing ___
4. Loosen grip ___
5. Keep racket face open ___

Execution

1. Hit at top of bounce ___
2. Hit down the back of the ball ___
3. Keep body still ___

Follow-Through

1. Control racket face ___
2. Grip racket more tightly ___

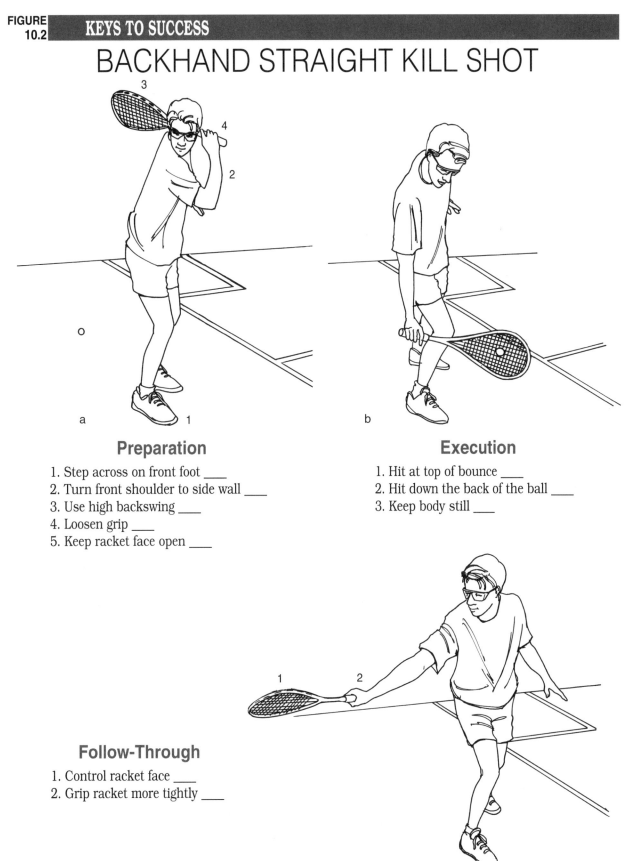

FIGURE 10.2

KEYS TO SUCCESS

BACKHAND STRAIGHT KILL SHOT

Preparation

1. Step across on front foot ___
2. Turn front shoulder to side wall ___
3. Use high backswing ___
4. Loosen grip ___
5. Keep racket face open ___

Execution

1. Hit at top of bounce ___
2. Hit down the back of the ball ___
3. Keep body still ___

Follow-Through

1. Control racket face ___
2. Grip racket more tightly ___

How to Perform the Crosscourt Kill

You should normally attempt the crosscourt kill only in the front half of the court. This shot is easier to hit than the straight kill, but beware; if your opponent can get the ball back you'll find yourself badly out of position.

You can play the shot in two ways. You can aim the ball straight for the side-wall nick after hitting the front wall, or you can aim it to bounce twice before reaching the side wall. Players more frequently go for the nick. Make sure, though, that if you miss the nick you at least hit the side wall first. This will keep the ball lower, making the return more difficult. Hit the ball out in front of you (see figure 10.3a). Again, take the ball early, hitting it close to the top of the bounce so that you can hit the ball down toward the nick. You normally attempt the second way when you're up close to the front wall. You can increase the effectiveness by "holding the shot" and trying to send your opponent the wrong way. Holding the shot means to wait with your racket prepared until the very last instant before swinging at the ball. The hope is that this will cause your opponent to move before he or she actually knows where you plan to hit the ball. With both shots, control and slice are more important than just hitting the ball hard (see figure 10.3b).

FIGURE 10.3

KEYS TO SUCCESS

CROSSCOURT KILL

Preparation
1. Prepare racket early ___
2. Bend your knees ___
3. Keep racket face open ___

Execution
1. Hit ball out in front of you ___
2. Hit at top of bounce ___
3. Hit with slice ___
4. Control the swing ___
5. Aim to hit the nick or for the ball to bounce twice before reaching side wall ___

a

b

How to Perform the Volley Kill

Killing the ball on the volley is often easier because you can take the ball from higher in the air than you can after it bounces. You can hit volley kills from anywhere on the court, but again, the farther back in the court, the greater the risk. You can hit this shot straight or crosscourt.

Players often use the straight volley kill to intercept an opponent's crosscourt. This is especially effective on a crosscourt from the back because you will then send your opponent diagonally to the opposite corner. The straight volley kill is often hit as a reflex shot off an opponent's loose drive, so quick preparation is essential to have any hope of consistently hitting a winner. The faster the ball comes at you, the shorter the swing that is necessary. Off an opponent's hard shot take just a short backswing and punch the ball into the front corner (see figure

10.4a). Keep the wrist firm and the racket face open so that you slice the ball. If your opponent's shot has less pace, you'll need a larger backswing and a faster swing-through to generate some pace on the shot. If you have to reach up for the shot, you'll need to loosen your wrist slightly so that you can bring the ball down. Yet you must still try to control the racket face as you swing through (see figure 10.4b).

You normally play the crosscourt volley kill from head height or above, usually off a loose shot in the midcourt area. The crosscourt volley kill can be a particularly effective way of attacking a bad serve. Again, you should hit the shot with plenty of slice. The wrist needs to be slightly looser than it is for most other shots so that you can whip the racket face through quickly. Aim to hit the front wall and then the side-wall nick. If you should miss the nick you should at least hit the side wall before the floor so that the ball doesn't bounce up too much.

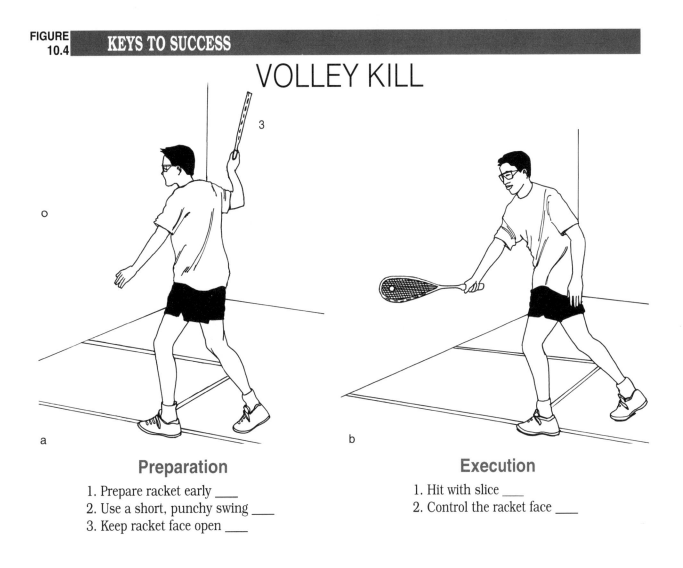

FIGURE 10.4

KEYS TO SUCCESS

VOLLEY KILL

a

Preparation

1. Prepare racket early ___
2. Use a short, punchy swing ___
3. Keep racket face open ___

b

Execution

1. Hit with slice ___
2. Control the racket face ___

KILL SHOT SUCCESS STOPPERS

You can tell when you are hitting good kill shots because your opponent won't be able to return the shot. If the majority of your kill shots aren't turning out to be winners, use the following list of corrections for common errors. Always remember, however, that you should be attempting kill shots only when you have worked a good opening.

Error	Correction
1. Your kill shots bounce up too much.	1. You need to hit your shot with more slice so that the ball dies more quickly after hitting the front wall. Open your racket face more and think about cutting down the back of the ball.
2. Your kill shots hit the tin.	2. Make sure that you hit the shot at the top of the bounce. If you let the ball drop as far as you would for a drive, it will be difficult to hit down on the ball and keep the ball from hitting the tin.
3. You have no control over your kill shots.	3. Keep your body still as you swing. Also, even though you are swinging through quickly, try to keep your racket face under control.

KILL SHOT

DRILLS

1. Racket Feed for Kill

Stand on the T. Hit a soft, high feed that bounces about halfway between the front wall and the short line. Step forward and hit a straight kill. Your feed should be at least a couple of feet away from the side wall so that you can try to angle the ball toward the nick. Remember to hit the ball at the top of the bounce and to hit with plenty of slice.

Success Goal =
5 out of 10 forehand kills hitting the nick ___
5 out of 10 backhand kills hitting the nick ___

To Increase Difficulty
• Stand farther back and hit kills from feeds that bounce in the service box.
• Feed the ball higher and hit straight volley kills.

Success Check
• Prepare the racket early and high ___
• Hit down the back of the ball ___
• Swing through quickly ___

2. Crosscourt Kills

Stand on the forehand side of the court about eight feet from the front wall and about five feet from the side wall. Turn your body so that you're facing the opposite side wall. Hit a backhand high on the opposite side wall so that it rebounds off the front wall and bounces between you and the front wall. Turn your body toward the front wall and prepare your racket for a forehand. Then, as the ball reaches the top of the bounce, hit a forehand crosscourt kill. Aim your shot to hit the nick. If the ball doesn't roll out of the nick, turn and try to feed again with the backhand without stopping. Repeat on the opposite side for backhand crosscourt kills.

 **Success Goal** =

5 out of 10 forehand kills hitting the nick ___
5 out of 10 backhand kills hitting the nick ___

 **To Increase Difficulty**

• Hit the feeds harder and lower.

✔ **Success Check**

• Keep the wrist loose ___
• Angle the ball toward the nick ___
• Bend your knees as you swing ___

3. Crosscourt Volley Kills

Stand on the T. Feed the ball with a backhand across your body so that it hits the front wall close to the side wall and then rebounds off the side wall back to you in the middle. Hit a forehand crosscourt volley kill. Make sure that you hit your kill shot far enough across the court so that if the ball doesn't hit the nick, it will at least hit the side wall before hitting the floor. If the ball bounces up enough, turn and feed the ball again without stopping. (Your goal, however, is to make the ball unretrievable.) After practicing forehand kills, hit forehand feeds for backhand crosscourt volley kills.

 **Success Goal** =

5 out of 10 forehand kills hitting the nick ___
5 out of 10 backhand kills hitting the nick ___

✔ **Success Check**

• Hit with plenty of slice ___
• Hit the ball in front of you ___
• Keep your feet still as you swing ___

To Increase Difficulty

• Hit the feeds harder to force yourself to prepare the racket more quickly.

To Decrease Difficulty

• Feed the ball more softly, let it bounce, and then hit a crosscourt kill.

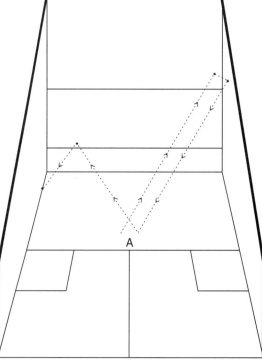

4. Kill Shot From Partner's Feed

Have a partner stand in the service box and feed the ball straight so that it bounces about halfway between the front wall and the short line. Move forward from the T and hit a straight kill shot. Try to hit your shot so that your partner can't return it. If the feed is close to the side wall, hit the ball tight to the side wall. If the feed is away from the side wall, angle your shot toward the nick.

**Success Goal** =
5 out of 10 unreturnable forehand kills ___
5 out of 10 unreturnable backhand kills ___

✔ Success Check
• Step across on front foot ___
• Turn front shoulder toward the side wall ___
• Hit the ball at the top of the bounce ___

To Increase Difficulty
• Hit crosscourt kills instead of straight kills.
• Have your partner feed higher on the front wall for you to hit volley kills.

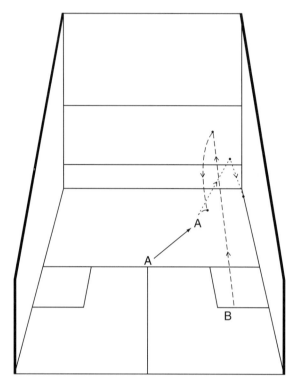

5. Frontcourt Game

Play a game with your opponent in which all shots must bounce in front of the short line. Begin each rally by serving from in front of the service box. The serve can be hit anywhere in the frontcourt but not for a winner. If you do win the rally off the serve, replay the point. Play point-per-rally scoring to 9 points. Encourage kill shots by awarding 2 points for any kill shot that hits the nick and is unreturnable.

Success Goal = Win 2 out of 3 games against your opponent ___

✔ Success Check
• Keep your racket face up ___
• Aim for the nick whenever possible ___
• Slice all your shots ___

To Increase Difficulty
• Draw a line closer to the front wall and play that the ball can't bounce beyond that line.

To Decrease Difficulty
• Play with the same rules except that your opponent can hit only straight shots.

6. Cutting Off Crosscourts

You and a partner should stand on the short line on opposite sides of the court. Your partner should hit a crosscourt drive, which you should cut off with a straight volley kill. After your kill shot, step forward and hit a crosscourt back for your partner to hit a straight volley kill. Don't worry if the ball bounces more than once before crosscourting. In fact, it's preferable that your volley kill be too good for you to reach before the second bounce.

 **Success Goal** = Keep drill going for 3 minutes ___

 **Success Check**
- Don't back up from the short line ___
- Prepare your racket early ___
- Use a short swing ___

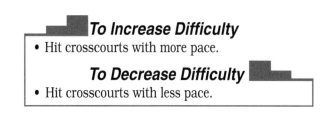 **To Increase Difficulty**
- Hit crosscourts with more pace.

To Decrease Difficulty
- Hit crosscourts with less pace.

7. Two Ball Feeds for Kill

Two feeders stand in the service boxes and alternately feed straight shots that bounce about halfway between the front wall and the short line. You move from side to side hitting straight kill shots. Have your partners count how many of your shots they couldn't get their racket face on before the ball bounced twice.

Success Goal = 20 unreturnable shots in 3 minutes ___

Success Check
- Side step across the court ___
- Prepare your racket early ___
- Hit down on the ball ___

To Increase Difficulty
- Have the feeders feed faster, forcing you to move more quickly.

To Decrease Difficulty
- Have the feeders feed only when you have turned and are ready for the shot.

KILL SHOT SUCCESS SUMMARY

Without a well-developed kill shot, you'll struggle to win rallies off an opponent's loose shots. The only way you'll be able to win is by wearing down your opponent. With the kill shot you can take advantage of a loose ball by hitting it low onto the front wall so that it dies in the nick. Never attempt a kill when feeling rushed or when cramped in the back corners. This shot requires much practice before you use it in a match situation; you have limited room for error. Again, have a partner watch you practice to check your stroke against the Keys to Success checklists in figures 10.1 through 10.4.

STEP 11

DISGUISE AND DECEPTION: KEEPING YOUR OPPONENT GUESSING

In previous steps we looked at two ways of applying pressure on your opponent. One way was to volley, and the second way was to kill the ball. We'll now consider a third way—using disguise and deception to send your opponent the wrong way (that is, to "wrong foot" your opponent) or at least keep your opponent guessing about where you're going to hit the ball, right up to the time you strike it.

Many players are under the misconception that disguise and deception are the same. This isn't true. *Disguise* is setting up for a shot in such a way that your opponent can't tell which shot you're about to play. *Deception* is setting up so that it looks as if you're going to play a particular shot, but you actually play another. When used effectively disguise and deception can unsettle your opponent because he or she is never sure which way to move.

Deception, when played well, can be devastating because it will be difficult for your opponent to keep from moving before you have struck the ball. Hitting with deception, however, requires that you use your wrist, and you'll often have to hit from an awkward body position. You thus risk hitting a weak shot. You should bring deception into your game slowly, experimenting with different racket preparations and body positions to see what works. Don't overdo it, though. Subtle changes will often completely fool your opponent, but exaggerated changes immediately signal your opponent to watch the ball, not your body or racket.

Why Is Disguise Important?

As you begin to play at higher levels, you'll find that your opponents are skillful at reading where you're going to hit the ball. You need to develop disguise to stop them from anticipating your shot and pouncing on the ball before you've had a chance to recover. If you disguise your shots, your opponent must wait on the T until you've hit the ball or risk moving in the wrong direction, handing you an easy point.

Disguise

Top-level players use disguise constantly by preparing early and in a similar way for all shots. When advanced players have time, you'll find it almost impossible to read what shot they're going to play until they play it. Remember these points when trying to increase the disguise on your shots:

- *Hold the shot*—This means waiting until the last possible moment to strike the ball. Holding your shots can cause your opponent to commit to moving in a particular direction before he or she is sure where the ball is going.

- *Prepare the racket early*—As you begin to practice your shots in game situations, concentrate on preparing the racket early. This will help you hold your shots.

- *Be decisive*—Even though you hope your opponent has no idea where the ball is going, be sure you know where you want to hit it. Any indecision on your part could cause you to mis-hit the shot and lose the rally from a strong position.

Also realize that because all shots in squash are variations of the basic swing, you'll inherently build disguise into your game as your stroke production improves. So work constantly on the basics of your technique.

Why Is Deception Important?

In the middle of a close match winning a point can be like climbing a mountain. If you match up evenly against your opponent, it helps to have some tricks up your sleeve to pull out during crucial rallies. Deception will give you this edge because, like the kill shot, it often leads to outright winners or at least puts your opponent well out of position. Deception has an advantage over the kill shot because even if you don't hit the shot perfectly (a frequent occurrence during tight matches) it's less likely to hit the tin.

Deception

You should bring deception into your match play slowly, improvising now and again with different body movements and hitting the ball from different positions in relation to your body. Use it sparingly, always keeping in mind that if you try to deceive your opponent too many times in the same way, he or she will catch on and start reading what you're going to do.

Attempt deception in match situations only after you've practiced and become comfortable with the shots. First, experiment on your own with different racket and body positions. At this stage you shouldn't hesitate to try anything. In game situations, however, you should limit yourself to hitting deception shots that you feel comfortable with. Here are several examples of deception shots used in match play.

Example 1

At the front of the court, set up for a drop shot with a short backswing and the racket face low (see figure 11.1a). Hold the shot as long as possible. As your opponent starts to move forward use the wrist to hit a hard crosscourt drive (see figure 11.1b).

Example 2

Set up with your body facing the front wall instead of the side wall, making it look as if you're going to hit crosscourt (see figure 11.2 a). Instead, punch the ball as hard as you can straight down the wall (see figure 11.2b). Turning your head toward the middle of the court as you strike the ball (the no-look shot) will add to the deception.

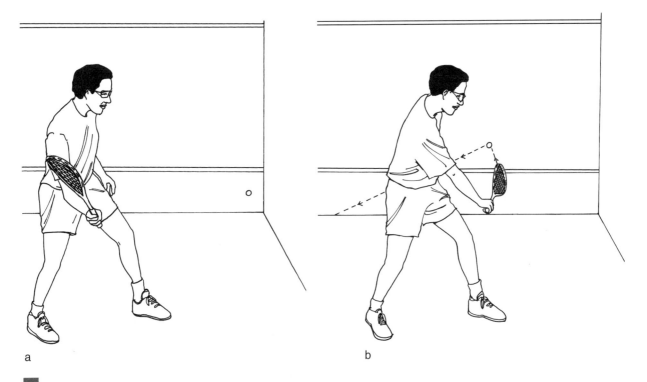

a   b

Figure 11.1 Preparing for a straight drop (a), then hitting a crosscourt drive (b).

a   b

Figure 11.2   Preparing for a crosscourt drive (a), then hitting a straight drive (b).

Example 3

In the back corner, turn your body so that you're facing the back wall as if you're going to play a boast (see figure 11.3a). Wait for the ball to come as far off the back wall as possible and drive the ball straight down the wall. Use a little wrist if necessary (see figure 11.3b).

Example 4

Set up for a straight drive (anywhere in the court) with the racket up early and high. Wait for the ball to come to your side, or even slightly behind you, to make it seem as if you could only play a straight drive or boast. Then, as you swing through, flick the wrist to send the ball crosscourt.

a   b

Figure 11.3   Preparing for a boast (a), then hitting a straight drive (b).

DISGUISE AND DECEPTION

DRILLS

Besides the drills that follow, you can use many other drills in this book to practice deception and disguise. The drills involving more than one person provide you an opportunity to hit with various racket preparations and body positions. Use the drills that offer you a choice of shots to see if you can wrong foot your partner.

1. Straight or Crosscourt?

Your partner stands in the backcourt and hits a boast. You move forward from the T and hit either a straight or crosscourt drive. Try to use disguise or deception to wrong foot your partner. Your partner should watch carefully and try to keep the drill going by returning your shot with another boast.

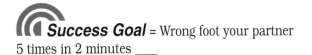 **Success Goal** = Wrong foot your partner 5 times in 2 minutes ___

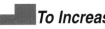 **Success Check**
• Hold your shots ___
• Use different body positions ___
• Use your wrist ___

To Increase Difficulty
• Allow your partner to hit drops or boasts.
• Confine your crosscourt shot to a lob.

2. Crosscourt or Drop?

Your partner stands in a back corner and hits a boast. You stand in the front corner and hit either a straight drop or a crosscourt drive. Your partner should move up to the T after the boast and try to return your crosscourt with a boast or your drop with another drop. Your goal is to hit your shot with as much deception as possible, trying to wrong foot your opponent. Play this as a game. You score a point if your shot is unreturnable, and your partner scores a point by successfully returning your shot.

Success Goal = Score 9 points before your partner does ___

Success Check
• Use a short backswing ___
• Hold your shot ___
• Use the wrist on the crosscourt ___

To Increase Difficulty
• Have your partner hit either a boast or a straight drop.

To Decrease Difficulty
• Have your partner hit a straight drop instead of a boast.

3. Deceive With the Boast

With a partner, play a rally in the back corner, hitting straight drives and circling around each other as in drill 4 of step 5. You are also allowed to use boasts but use them sparingly. Hit with disguise and deception to try to send your opponent the wrong way. Play as a game in which the drives must hit beyond the short line and no farther from the side wall than the width of the service box. If you play a boast that your partner is unable to return, you win the point. Your partner scores a point by returning the boast (with any shot).

 **Success Goal =**

Score 9 points on the forehand side before your partner does ___

Score 9 points on the backhand side before your partner does ___

To Increase Difficulty

• Allow your partner to hit a boast shot too.

 **Success Check**

• Prepare racket high ___
• Wait as long as possible before striking the ball ___
• Use same body position for both boasts and drives ___

DISGUISE AND DECEPTION SUCCESS SUMMARY

After you have a firm grasp of the basics of good stroke production and movement, you're ready to elevate your play in other ways. To keep good players from anticipating your shots, you need to develop tactics of disguise and deception. While these two aspects differ from one another, you use both to keep your opponent guessing throughout the match. With disguise, make no definite racket or position moves until the last moment, but be sure you know where you want to hit the ball. With deception, you must be ready to use more wrist than normal to direct the ball in ways other than indicated by your racket and body position. These techniques require a great deal of experimentation and practice. You should use them sparingly.

STEP
12
MATCH PLAY: PREPARING MENTALLY AND PHYSICALLY

Learning good technique and movement will certainly help you on your path toward excelling at squash. But when you watch a squash match you'll often see a player with superior shot play and fitness lose. This occurs because the opponent prepared better for the match and is more knowledgeable about strategic play. Shot selection in squash is critical. Having good technique isn't worth much if you play the wrong shot in a particular situation and leave yourself helplessly out of position. Good strategy comes from being well prepared and having some basic principles to fall back on in times of need.

When you step on court to begin a match, think about trying to establish your basic game. This involves pinning your opponent into the back corners with solid drives. Once you establish your basic game begin to hit more to the frontcourt to work your opponent around the court. Always remember the three basic good habits:

- Watch the ball.
- Move to the T.
- Prepare your racket early.

Remember that if things aren't going your way, you should try something different to break your opponent's rhythm.

Match Preparation

It's important to develop a prematch routine that will allow you to step on court in a relaxed, yet focused, manner. Arrive for your match in plenty of time to change, warm up, and check which court you're playing on. This last point is particularly important if you're playing at a club for the first time or if you're

playing in a tournament where you may not learn your court assignment until you arrive at the club. Allow at least 15 minutes to warm up. During this time begin to focus on the match. Positive thinking at this stage, particularly if you're nervous about the upcoming match, can help you get into the right mind-set for the game. Check out the court conditions because the temperature will affect the bounce of the ball. If the court is hot you can expect a match with long, drawn-out rallies. You'll need to be prepared to concentrate for long periods to avoid making unforced errors. If the court is cold the ball is likely to be slower and the rallies shorter. In this situation you should be ready to play very tight squash. Any loose shots will be easily dispatched for winners by your opponent. Make full use of the five-minute on court warm-up period to groove your strokes and check out your opponent.

Establish Your Basic Game

Once the match begins your main priority should be to establish your basic game—hitting good, solid drives deep into the back corners. This should help settle your nerves and get you into the rhythm of the game. Make your opponent work for the first few points; don't hit too many shots to the frontcourt where you risk making errors. Nothing is worse than falling quickly behind in the first game by making a series of unforced errors. Also, early on in the match your opponent will be fresh and able to run down your shots to the front corners. If you can keep your opponent on his or her heels at the back of the court, your frontcourt shots later in the match will be more effective.

Work Your Opponent Around the Court

Once you have established your basic game, you should begin to introduce more shots to the frontcourt to move your opponent up and down the court. In particular, look for opportunities to move your opponent from one back corner to the opposite front corner and vice versa. Do this, for example, by pushing your opponent forward with a drop and then driving the return to the opposite back corner. Or cut out one of your opponent's drives from the back with a drop volley or a boast.

Try to get away from the idea of hitting outright winners. Instead, look for combinations of shots to put your opponent so out of position that you can win the point by hitting to the open court.

Change a Losing Game

The old adage "never change a winning game, but always change a losing one" definitely applies to squash. If you're winning keep plugging away with the same strategy. You don't want to risk giving away the winning position by changing your strategy. On the other hand, if you're losing you must try different tactics to break your opponent's rhythm. One particularly good strategy is to change the pace of the game. Slow the game down by hitting more lobs, or, if the game is already at a slow pace, speed it up by volleying more and hitting harder drives. You could also change the game by trying to attack more. If you're losing because you're making too many mistakes, try to extend the rallies by hitting more to the back of the court.

One situation in which you may not want to change strategy when losing is when you're playing a clearly superior opponent. In this type of match, don't become disheartened. Instead, look at the match as a challenge and a way of improving your game. Try not to give your opponent easy points by constantly going for winners. Keep the rallies going as long as you can, making your opponent work hard for each point. You may find that by doing this you lose by a larger margin, but you should be able to keep your opponent on court longer. In the long run this will be more beneficial to your game.

Maintain Your Composure

Squash is a game that can test your mental patience to the limit. In the heat of battle it is easy to let a few breaks that go against you, such as a referee's call or a lucky shot from your opponent, upset you and hence cause you to lose concentration. It is important when you play to focus on your own game and try to ignore external factors as much as possible. Rarely will external factors determine the outcome of a match unless you allow them to. So concentrate all your effort on what you can control.

Showing anger toward the referee or your opponent is also extremely unsportsmanlike. Remember that normally the referee is working voluntarily and is doing the best job he or she can. Also, squash should be fun for you and your opponent. It is not much fun playing against someone who is constantly ranting and raving. So try to keep your emotions to yourself, stay composed, and concentrate on the match at hand.

Foster the Three Most Important Habits

Squash is a difficult game to master. Improvement often takes much time and practice. So you should gradually try to incorporate some of the ideas discussed in this book about stroke production and movement. Trying to do too much too quickly, however, may have a negative effect on your game. So begin by fostering three basic good habits:

1. Watch the ball. This is particularly important when your opponent is hitting out of the back corners. Don't stare at the front wall; turn and watch your opponent strike the ball. This will give you the time you need to retrieve the shot.

2. Move to the T. After you've played your shot, don't just stand waiting until your opponent hits the ball. Instead, move to the T so you can cover all four corners.

3. Prepare the racket early. As soon as you decide whether you're going to hit a forehand or a backhand, begin to prepare the racket. Getting the racket back early will help you move into the correct position to hit the ball and will give you more time to get to your opponent's shots.

MATCH PLAY

DRILLS

1. Pressure Drills

Have a partner stand in the back corner and hit either boasts, drops, or straight drives. From the T, move to the ball and drive it back to your partner. This exercise puts you under the sort of pressure you might face in your toughest matches. Keep the drill going as long as you can, using the lob to slow down the exercise if necessary.

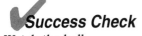 **Success Goal** = Keep the exercise going for 5 minutes ___

Success Check
• Watch the ball ___
• Recover to the T ___
• Lob when under pressure ___

To Increase Difficulty
• Have your partner stand in the backcourt hitting boasts, drops, or drives. You must hit only straight drives.

To Decrease Difficulty
• Have your partner hit only drops or drives, no boasts.
• Have your partner alternate hitting boast, drop, and drive, in that order.

2. Conditioned Backcourt Game

Play a conditioned game in which your opponent can play any shot, but you must hit all your shots to bounce past the short line. You may find yourself struggling to win rallies against a strong partner. Try to set realistic targets. If you aren't winning many points concentrate on keeping the rallies going. Play one game to 15 points with point-per-rally scoring.

 **Success Goal** = Score 7 points against your opponent ___

Success Check
• Concentrate on good width ___
• Keep changing the pace ___
• Try to be patient ___

To Increase Difficulty
• Besides hitting all your shots past the short line, you must hit all your shots straight.

To Decrease Difficulty
• You must hit all shots past the short line except for one type of shot. For example, hit all shots past the short line except for the forehand boast, which can bounce in front of the short line.

3. Conditioned Volley Game

Play a conditioned game in which you must not let the ball hit the back wall. If it does, you immediately lose the point. During this game you must stay alert and prepare the racket early so you can cut off your opponent's shots in the midcourt area. Also, the deeper in the court you keep your opponent, the harder you make it for your opponent to drive the ball past you. Play one game to 15 points with point-per-rally scoring.

((Success Goal = Score 7 points against your opponent ___

To Decrease Difficulty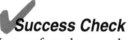
- Have your opponent play with the same shot restriction.

✔ Success Check
- Prepare your racket early ___
- Volley at every opportunity ___
- Keep your opponent deep ___

4. Short Handicap Games

The object of these games is to put you into the pressure of end-of-game situations. Play a game to 5 points with point-per-rally scoring. The player who loses the game begins the next game a point ahead (at 1-0). If the same player loses the next game, he or she starts the third game 2 points ahead. If that player wins, the score reverts to 0-0. Keep playing games in this fashion. If a player already starts a game at 3-0 and loses, then the player who won the game starts the next game with –1 (negative 1). If you know at the start that you and your partner differ in ability, you may want to begin the first game with the weaker player leading by whatever you agree is an appropriate margin.

((Success Goal = Win more games than your opponent ___

✔ Success Check
- Keep unforced errors down to a minimum ___
- Play every rally as if you are game point down ___
- Establish a strong basic game ___

5. Three-Quarter Court

Play a rally in which one of the back quarters of the court is out of court. You can play this game with any number of players. The players not involved in the rally line up in the back corner, which isn't in play. The winner of the rally stays on and receives in the next rally. The loser of the rally joins the end of the line, and the player at the front of the line serves in the next rally. Keep score, 1 point for every rally you win. Play until one player reaches 15 points. Then switch sides so the opposite back corner is out of court.

 **Success Goal** = Score 15 points before your opponents ___

✔ **Success Check**
• Watch the ball ___
• Move to the T ___
• Prepare your racket early ___

To Increase Difficulty
• Instead of using three-quarters of the court use only one-half (either the forehand side or the backhand side).

MATCH PLAY SUCCESS SUMMARY

The culmination of all your basic learning comes with match and tournament play. Yet the player who doesn't prepare properly for a match or doesn't choose shots wisely during the match can waste strong fundamentals. Always remember the habits to foster on the squash court—watch the ball, prepare your racket early, and move back to the T after each shot. The only way to get comfortable playing under match conditions is to go out and play. When playing tournaments, keep in mind that you and your opponent should be having fun. Maintaining a sportsmanlike attitude on the court will help ensure this.

RATING YOUR PROGRESS

Rate your progress by writing the appropriate number in the space to the right of each skill. Add the numbers when you finish and check the key that follows to get an indication of your progress.

5 = Excellent   **4** = Above average   **3** = Average   **2** = Below average   **1** = Unsuccessful

1. Grip _____
2. Handling the racket _____
3. Forehand swing _____
4. Backhand swing _____
5. Moving to the front corners _____
6. Drives from the front corners _____
7. Moving to the back corners _____
8. Drives from the back corners _____
9. Volley _____
10. Serve _____
11. Return of serve _____

12. Boast _____
13. Drop shot _____
14. Lob _____
15. Kill shot _____
16. Disguise _____
17. Deception _____
18. Establishing basic game _____
19. Moving to the T _____
20. Preparing the racket early _____
21. Watching the ball _____
22. Moving opponent around court _____

Total _____

Score	Progress
100-110	Excellent
90-100	Above average
80-90	Average
Less than 80	Below average

You can use these ratings for each skill as a method to assess which steps you need to work on the most. This is particularly useful for helping you plan which drills to concentrate on.

Even when your rating reaches the "Excellent" level, don't think that your work is done. There's always room for improvement!

APPENDIX: MOST INFLUENTIAL PLAYERS

The following is a list of the players who have had the greatest influence on the game of squash. Putting together such a list as this obviously invites controversy. Clearly, other players influenced the game at different times as well. But the players listed here are pivotal because all of them dominated the game and shaped it into the action-packed mixture of shot play and fitness that it is today. This is, however, a very subjective list based on accounts of matches from numerous people who have reported on the games.

F. D. Amr Bey (Egypt)

Abdel Fattah Amr, known as F.D. Amr Bey, moved to England in 1928 as an Egyptian diplomat. At that time his main sports were tennis and polo, and he represented Egypt at tennis in the Davis Cup. Once introduced to squash, he took to the game quickly. Building on his natural racket ability, he developed the speed and strength to adapt to the more rigorous game of squash. He introduced a wide range of strokes to the game, which combined with his athleticism made for a game of precision and endurance.

It took only a couple of years for Amr to begin to make an impact on the squash scene. He won his first major tournament in 1931, beating the Englishman Dugald Macpherson in a five-game final of the British Amateur Championships. This was followed the next year by winning the British Open (the unofficial world championships) over then-current champion Don Butcher. At that time the British Open was decided on a challenge basis. The reigning champion had to face a challenge over a three-match series. Butcher had won the first two years of the tournament, but was now no match for Amr. Amr won the first match comfortably and despite dropping the first two games of the second match, he secured the next three with the loss of only three points to make a third match unnecessary. Amr did not receive a challenge in 1933 and then went on, from 1934 through 1937, to complete four more consecutive wins against challenges from Butcher and Jim Dear. During this same period he won six British Amateur Championships and was the only player other than Jonah Barrington to win both titles in the same year, a feat he actually accomplished on five occasions.

Sadly for the squash world, Amr retired in 1938 at the age of 28 while still the top player in the game to pursue his career as a diplomat. He went on to become the Egyptian ambassador to the United Kingdom.

Hashim Khan (Pakistan)

Hashim Khan began a period in the 1950s and early 1960s that was dominated by the "Khan clan." From 1950 to 1962, the British Open was won by either Hashim, his brother Azam Khan, his cousin Roshan Khan, or Azam's nephew, Mohibullah Khan.

Hashim was the first player to choke up on the racket, a grip he adopted at an early age due to his small stature. With this grip he was able to develop masterful control over the racket face and a wide variety of exotic shots. He dominated squash in Pakistan and came to England in 1950. He easily defeated the then-current champion, Egyptian Mahmoud Khan, in the final of the British Open by a 9-5, 9-0, 9-0 score. Remarkably, Hashim was 35 to 37 years old (his exact birth date is unknown) when he won his first British Open, but he went on to win the title a total of seven times in the next eight years.

He moved to America and dominated the hard-ball game, but returned to England each year from 1977 to 1982 to win a record six straight British Open Vintage (for players 55 years and older) titles, the last of which he won at the approximate age of 69.

Janet Shardlow (England)

Janet Shardlow dominated the women's squash scene in the 1950s, winning 10 consecutive British Open championships between 1949 and 1958 before she was forced to retire due to a back injury. Shardlow was another player who was introduced to squash via tennis. She played 14 times in the Wimbledon tennis championships and represented England in the Wightman Cup. She took up squash in 1946 at the age of 24. It took only two years for her to reach her first British Open final, where she was beaten 10-8 in the fifth game by Jean Curry. Curry beat her in the final the following year as well, but then Shardlow began her period of domination. She dominated the British Open so thoroughly during this 10-year period that she dropped a total of only seven games and only once looked like she might be about to lose when she had to recover from a two-game deficit against Fran Marshall in the 1957 semifinal.

Shardlow was responsible for popularizing squash for women in Australia and New Zealand when she toured these countries in 1954. Ironically, Australian Heather McKay would go on to overshadow Shardlow's domination and eclipse her record 10 consecutive wins.

Heather McKay (Australia)

Heather McKay was undoubtedly the greatest woman squash player ever. Her record in squash outshines that of virtually any other person in any sport. After losing to Fran Marshall in the final of the Scottish Open in January 1962, she was never to lose a competitive match again. She won 16 straight British Open championships, dropping a total of only two games. In the 1968 final she beat fellow Australian Bev Johnson 9-0, 9-0, 9-0, the only time this has happened in the history of the tournament. Johnson should gain some comfort from the fact that McKay had already demolished her semifinal opponent by the same score line and her quarterfinal opponent with the loss of only two points. In addition to her British Open successes, she won 14 Australian National Championships and won the first ever Women's World Championships in Brisbane in 1976, and returned later in 1979 to regain the title.

McKay grew up in New South Wales, Australia, and took up squash in 1959 at the age of 17. She came to England in 1962 after winning the Australian National Championship for the first time. She married her husband Brian in 1965 and they moved to Canada in 1975. Once there, McKay retired from squash to take up the more lucrative sport of racquetball.

Jonah Barrington (Ireland)

Jonah Barrington brought a new dimension to the squash world—the ability to win by physically outlasting your opponent. He was a late starter to the game, not playing his first squash match until he was 23 years old. But he had an unparalleled dedication. He trained unmercifully and constantly pestered better players to play him. Soon, Barrington developed such physical fitness that he began to beat these same players by wearing them into the ground.

In 1966 he became the second player to win both the British Amateur Championship and British Open in the same year. He was also the first British player to win the British Open since Jim Dear in 1939. Barrington would go on to win the British Open six times and the British Amateur Championship three times.

Barrington was responsible for forcing all professional squash players to concentrate on fitness. It would now be almost impossible to compete at the top level on shot-making ability alone. Barrington was also such a charismatic person that he was practically single-handedly responsible for the widespread growth of squash in the 1970s.

Barrington reached at least the quarterfinals of the British Open 15 times from 1966 to 1981. Also during that time span he never lost to a British player despite the slew of talented young players then emerging on the British squash scene.

After his retirement from the professional playing scene in 1982 he continued to play in age-group events and to coach the British National Junior Squads.

Geoff Hunt (Australia)

As Jonah Barrington began to fade, the mantle passed to a mild-mannered yet extremely determined Australian named Geoff Hunt. Hunt had a wider variety of shots than Barrington but, at least at first, lacked the Irishman's fitness. This led to some classic confrontations as Hunt tried to put Barrington away before fatigue set in. Initially, Barrington had the upper hand with two British Open final victories against Hunt, including a brutal 9-7 in the fifth match in the 1971 tournament. Eventually, however, Hunt's improving fitness level soon was on a par with and then surpassed that of Barrington, but he was left to face the challenge of a host of Pakistani players.

Hunt won his first British Open in 1973 when Mohammed Yasin had to withdraw before the final due to injury. After the creative shot maker Qamar Zaman took the title in 1974, Hunt went on a run of seven consecutive Open wins to set a new record of eight titles.

Hunt had a knack for winning games from the brink of defeat, which was particularly frustrating for Zaman, who failed on countless occasions to topple the Australian. Hunt's record eighth British Open title came in 1981 against the 17-year-old Jahangir Khan. It was a remarkable achievement for Hunt to subdue the highly talented youngster, but it was to be his last major victory. Jahangir would beat Hunt in the final of the 1981 World Open to end Hunt's run of four World Open titles (these were the first four World Opens to be held).

Hunt retired in 1982 due to a cracked vertebra. He later had surgery on his back and made a brief comeback, but he spent most of his time coaching at the Australian Institute of Sport where he helped to develop an impressive array of young Australian players, including Rodney and Brett Martin, Chris Dittmar, and Rodney Eyles.

Vicki Cardwell (Australia)

Heather McKay's retirement opened up women's squash for other players to win major tournaments. At first, no one had a firm grasp on the number-one spot until Vicki Cardwell powered her way to the forefront of the women's game by capturing the 1980 British Open.

Cardwell was a short, stocky, hard-hitting Australian. She was aggressive on the court and extremely competitive. She would go on to capture the next three British Open titles, but her inexplicable failure in the 1981 World Open, losing 9-7 in the fifth game of the final to Rhonda Thorne, would not sit well with her. In 1983 (the World Open is held on a biannual basis) she would make amends. The tournament, held in Perth, Australia, was to be her defining moment. She powered her way through the draw without dropping a game, including a reversal of the result of the previous final against Thorne where she won comfortably 9-1, 9-3, 9-4.

With the World Open crown now hers, she retired happily to start a family with husband Ian. She did return to the sport a few years later, briefly climbing her way back into the top five in the world, although Susan Devoy was to see to it that Cardwell would not recapture any of the major titles.

Jahangir Khan (Pakistan)

Jahangir Khan was the best of the next generation of the "Khan clan." He was the son of Roshan Khan, the British Open winner in 1956, and nephew of the great Hashim Khan. Jahangir's brother Torsam was also a great squash player, making it to the top 10 in the world before tragically dying on court during a match in Adelaide, Australia. This tragic incident early in Jahangir's career served as inspiration to Jahangir to work even harder to become the best squash player ever.

Jahangir's achievements were remarkable not only for their magnitude but also because they came while he was still at such a young age. He won the 1978 World Amateur Championships at only 15 years of age. He joined the professional scene in 1980, and by the end of 1981 was number one in the world. Jahangir produced countless upsets during that first season as a professional, including a fine win against Geoff Hunt in the Chichester Festival. This set up a fascinating rematch two weeks later in the final of the British Open. Jahangir looked on his way to repeating his earlier victory when he won the third game after dropping the first two games and then took a 6-2 lead in the fourth. Hunt, however, was not to be denied and astoundingly found the energy necessary to come back and win the fourth game 9-7 and with it the match. This disappointment would be Jahangir's last for a long while. He would beat Hunt in the final of the World Open later in 1981 and then, with Hunt's retirement, would begin a streak of remarkable dominance.

Not only could Jahangir match the fitness level of Barrington and the stroke play and mental toughness of Hunt, but he had awesome power. He was simply relentless on the court, attacking opponents with a barrage of well-executed, hard-hit shots. His opponents found themselves under constant pressure with no time to settle into normal game plans. After the British Open loss to Hunt, Jahangir would not lose another match for over five and a half years. During this time he won five British Opens, five World Opens, close to 100 other major tournaments, and nearly 500 successive matches!

There were only two players who could even stretch Jahangir during this spell. The first was Gamal Awad, an Egyptian who began to push Jahangir during the 1982–83 season. This culminated in the longest-ever squash match in the final of the Chichester Festival. The match lasted 2 hours and 45 minutes before Jahangir came out the victor, 3-1. The effort put forth by Gamal in this match was to prove fatal for Gamal's squash game. He made it to the final of the British Open a few weeks later but then began to slip down the rankings and never seriously challenged Jahangir again. The next major challenge to Jahangir came from New Zealand's Ross Norman. In the 15 months prior to the 1986 World Open final Norman would lose to Jahangir in eight consecutive major finals. Finally in Toulouse on November 11, 1986, Norman would have his day. He beat Jahangir 3-1 to lift the World Open crown and end Jahangir's astonishing run. Again, the effort put forward by Jahangir's challenger would take its toll. Norman remained in the top ranks of the game for 10 more years but would never come close to repeating his victory against Jahangir.

Norman's victory began to give other players more confidence against Jahangir. In the 1987 British Open semifinal, Rodney Martin stood on the verge of victory when he led two games to love and 6-4 in the third. Jahangir would eventually hold off Martin to win in five games in what was arguably the finest match in British Open history. Jahangir would win the final comfortably against an upcoming Pakistani named Jansher Khan (incidentally, no relation). Jansher, however, would prove to be a thorn in Jahangir's side for the following four years.

The two Khans could not be less alike. Jahangir was the perfect professional—quiet, well-mannered, a perfect ambassador of the game. Jansher was brash and controversial. His lack of respect for Jahangir offended the world number-one and fueled a bitter on-court rivalry. Jahangir had problems overcoming Jansher's game plan of slowing down the pace of the game and breaking up Jahangir's attacking play. Jansher beat Jahangir in the semifinal of the 1987 World Open, but Jahangir would retain the title by beating Jansher in the final the following year. This would be Jahangir's last World Open victory as he fixed his sights instead on topping Geoff Hunt's eight British Open wins. Each year Jahangir would come to the British Open focused and in peak condition. He was unstoppable in this tournament and went on to a record 10 consecutive wins between 1982 and 1991.

Injury would force Jahangir out of the 1992 British Open and into retirement. He made a brief return in 1993 to compete in the World Open in Pakistan. He made it to the final to set up one last encounter with Jansher. Jansher would win this match 3-1 to bring the Jahangir era to a close.

Susan Devoy (New Zealand)

Vicki Cardwell's retirement looked like it would finally open the door for Britain's Lisa Opie. Opie had lost in the 1982 and 1983 finals, and when she reached the final in 1984, with Cardwell's absence, most observers felt it would be third-time lucky. But nobody was counting on a young New Zealander named Susan Devoy stepping up to take center stage. After dropping the first game, she powered her way through the next three to win her first British Open title.

Devoy moved to England as an 18-year-old in 1982. Under the guidance of top New Zealand coach Bryce Taylor, she made a quick surge up the world rankings and became the first New Zealander to win a British Open. Devoy had great speed around the court and an aggressive attacking game. Her most potent weapon, however, was her backhand drop shot, which she used in combination with hard-hit drives to keep her opponents constantly moving up and down the court.

Devoy would dominate the women's game from 1984 to 1992. During that period she won eight out of nine British Opens and four out of five World Opens. Her only defeats in the two major tournaments came in the quarterfinal of the

1991 British Open, where she was surprisingly beaten by Sue Wright; and in the final of the 1989 World Open, where she was beaten by Martine Le Moignan. These blemishes on her record were far surpassed by her dominating performances as she kept at bay a large number of hungry British challengers including Opie, Le Moignan, Suzzane Horner and Lucy Soutter, as well as a crop of talented Australians led by Liz Irving, Michelle Martin, and Sarah Fitzgerald.

Jansher Khan (Pakistan)

Jansher Khan is the current world number-one. He has dominated the game since Jahangir Khan began to fade from the squash scene in 1992. Jansher first came to prominence in 1986 when he won the World Junior Championships. He followed this with an improbable run to the final of the 1987 British Open. At this time he was still only 17 years old, but he put together an astonishing run of outstanding performances, toppling three higher ranked opponents—Gawain Briars, Ross Norman, and Chris Dittmar—all in brutal five-game marathons. His run was finally ended by Jahangir in the final, which began an intense rivalry between the two Pakistani players.

The young Jansher was tall and lightly built. He lacked the power and variety of shots Jahangir owned, but he covered the court with exceptional speed and had an ability to slow the pace of a game down to disrupt his opponent's rhythm. The real asset that Jansher brought to the squash court, however, was a tremendous belief in his ability to win. At a time when Jahangir was beginning to look more vulnerable, Jansher was the only player who appeared to step on court knowing he could win. And in 1987, win he did—first in the Hong Kong Open, then on home soil in Pakistan, and finally in the World Open semifinal in England. Jansher went on to defeat Chris Dittmar in the final of that tournament to begin his record-breaking World Open supremacy. Jahangir would regain the World Open in 1988, but Jansher would win 1989 and 1990 and then five more times between 1992 and 1996.

Despite Jansher's success in the World Open, the British Open crown would elude him early in his career. He could not break Jahangir's lock on the tournament and would have to wait until 1992 (his sixth attempt) before capturing the title. Since this time Jansher has dominated this and every other tournament. He has currently won five British Open championships and in a five-year period from 1992 to 1996 he lost only four times in major competitions.

Jansher now relies less on his stamina to win matches. He has developed an impressive array of shots to complement his speed around the court. He trains less now than in his younger days in the hope that he can save his body enough to overhaul Jahangir's British Open record.

GLOSSARY

ace—A winning service when the receiver makes no contact with the ball.

all—Term used to describe a tie score; for example, 3-3 is "3 all."

American scoring—Another name for point-per-rally scoring; a scoring system in which games are played to 15, and points are scored regardless of who is serving.

appeal—A player's request to the referee to allow a let or to reconsider a decision just made.

angle—A shot that hits a side wall before hitting the front wall.

backcourt—The area of the court behind the short line.

backhand—A shot hit to the side of the body opposite the side on which the player holds the racket.

back quarter—The part of the court bounded by the side wall, back wall, half-court line, and short line. A served ball (if allowed by the receiver to bounce) must bounce within this area opposite the service box from which the ball was served.

back-wall boast—A shot hit against the back wall before hitting the front wall.

backswing—The player's initial movement with the racket in preparation for hitting the ball.

board—Another name for the tin, the area below the lowest horizontal line on the front wall.

boast—A shot that hits a side wall or the back wall before hitting the front wall.

British Open—A professional squash tournament in Britain, it was the unofficial world championship until 1976. Still regarded by many players as the premier squash tournament.

carry—An illegal shot in which a player holds or "carries" the ball on the racket strings.

choke up—To hold the racket higher, or closer to the racket face, on the racket handle.

conditioned game—A modified game in which the players can hit only certain shots or hit only to certain areas of the court.

consolation tournament—An event for first-round losers of a tournament.

crosscourt—A shot that lands in the opposite side of the court from which it was played.

cut line—The middle horizontal line on the front wall six feet above the floor. When serving, the player must hit the ball above this line.

deception—A player sets up as if to play a particular shot but then hits a different one in an attempt to wrong foot the opponent.

default—A player is awarded the match because the opponent fails to show up or is unable to compete.

die—An expression to describe a ball that stays close to the floor after bouncing because a player hit it softly, with slice, or in the nick, thus making it impossible to return.

disguise—A player sets up in such a way that the opponent is unable to tell what shot is going to be played.

down—The expression used to indicate that the ball hit the tin or failed to reach the front wall.

down the line—A shot hit straight along the side wall.

drive—A basic forehand or backhand shot hit after the bounce to one of the back corners.

drop—A shot hit softly onto the front wall so that the ball dies in the frontcourt.

double elimination—A tournament in which two losses eliminate a player or team.

error—When a player loses a point due to a mistake (for example, hitting the ball into the tin or out of court).

fault—An unsuccessful service.

final—The last match of a tournament played to determine the winner.

follow-through—The final part of the racket's swing after the player makes contact with the ball.

forehand—A shot hit on the side of the body on which the player holds the racket.

foot fault—An unsuccessful service due to the server not having at least one foot completely in the service box when making contact with the ball.

game—Part of the match that is completed when one player scores 9 points (in traditional scoring), 15 points (in point-per-rally scoring), or wins the tie break.

game ball—The state of the score when one player will win the game if he or she wins the next rally.

get—A successful return from a difficult position.

grip—The way that a player holds the racket.

half-court line—A line on the floor parallel to the side walls, dividing the backcourt equally into two parts. The line meets the short line at its midpoint to form the T.

halftime—Referee's call to signal the midpoint of the warm-up.

half volley—A shot played close to the floor immediately after the ball has bounced.

hand—The duration of a player's time while serving.

hand out—Referee's call to indicate that a change of server has occurred.

International Squash Rackets Federation (ISRF)—The governing body for squash worldwide.

kill shot—A shot that a player hits hard and low on the front wall so that it dies before the opponent has an opportunity to return it.

let—A situation in which a rally is replayed.

lob—A shot lofted high onto the front wall so that the ball arcs softly into the backcourt.

loose shot—A poor shot that bounces toward the middle of the court, giving the opponent the chance to hit a winner.

love—The term used for zero in the scoring system.

marker—Official that calls the score during a squash match.

match—Competition between two players, normally completed when one player wins three games.

match ball—The state of the score when one player will win the match by winning the next rally.

nick—The crack between the wall and the floor. If the ball hits one of these cracks it often rolls out, giving the player no opportunity to make a good return.

not up—Expression used to indicate that the player struck the ball after it bounced twice or the player struck the ball twice.

out—Expression used to indicate that the ball struck a wall on or above the out line, struck the ceiling, or struck or passed through any fitting hanging from the ceiling.

out line—A continuous line formed by a horizontal line on the front wall 15 feet above the floor, a horizontal line on the back wall 7 feet above the floor, and diagonal lines on the side walls connecting the lines on the front and back walls. On courts with glass back walls, if there is no line on the back wall the out line is considered to be the top of the glass.

penalty point—A situation in which a player wins a rally due to interference from the opponent.

Perspex court—A portable court with one-way-view walls that can be erected in large halls to accommodate larger audiences.

Philadelphia—A shot played from the frontcourt. The ball is hit high on the front wall, near the corner, so that it hits the near side wall and then travels diagonally across the court to the opposite back corner.

point-per-rally scoring—Scoring system in which games are played to 15 points, and points are scored regardless of who serves.

professional—A player who makes a living from playing or teaching squash.

Professional Squash Association (PSA)—The organization responsible for running the professional squash tournament circuit.

racket face—The hitting surface or strings of the racket.

rackets—A game that is similar to squash but is played on a large slate court with a small, hard ball.

rail—Another name for a drive hit down the line.

rally—An exchange of shots beginning with the service and ending when the ball ceases to be in play.

receiver—The player who is not serving at the beginning of a rally.

referee—Official responsible for adjudicating all decisions during a squash match.

reverse angle—A shot hit against the side wall farther from you.

round robin—A tournament in which a player or team will play against all the other players or teams. The winner is the player or team with the most wins.

server—The player who serves at the beginning of a rally.

service—The method by which a player puts the ball in play to begin a rally.

service box—Two squares on opposite sides of the court, just behind the short line, from which the server must serve.

set—The number of points the receiver chooses to play in a tie break at the end of a game. For example, in traditional scoring if the score reaches 8-8 the receiver can choose set one or set two. In point-per-rally scoring if the score reaches 14-14 the receiver can choose set one or set three.

short line—A line on the floor parallel to the front and back walls, 18 feet from the front wall.

single elimination—A tournament in which a loss eliminates a player or team.

skid boast—A shot hit from the backcourt. The ball is hit up on the side wall so that it strikes high in the center of the front wall and then travels to the opposite back corner.

slice—To hit the ball with spin (that is, with an open racket face) so that the ball stays lower after it hits the front wall.

stroke—A situation in which a player wins a rally because of interference from the opponent.

sweet spot—The place on the racket face that produces the most power.

T—The line configuration in the middle of the court formed by the short line and the half-court line.

tie break—In traditional scoring, the state of the game when the score reaches 8-8. The receiver must choose either set one or set two. In point-per-rally scoring it is the state of the game when the score reaches 14-14. Here the receiver must choose either set one or set three.

tin—A metal strip 19 inches high at the bottom of the front wall.

traditional scoring—Scoring system in which games are played to 9 points, and only the server can score points.

trickle boast—A shot hit from the frontcourt that hits the side wall before hitting the front wall.

turning on the ball—Name given to the situation in which a player makes a 180-degree turn in the back of the court and hits the ball with the forehand on the backhand side or vice versa.

United States Squash Racquets Association (USSRA)—The governing body for squash in the United States.

volley—A shot hit before the ball has bounced on the floor.

warm-up—A five-minute period before the start of a match to allow players to practice and to warm up the ball.

winner—A shot that the opponent cannot return.

wrong foot—A term used to describe when a player mistakenly moves in a different direction than where the ball was hit.

yellow dot—The color of the dot on the slowest-speed squash ball. The yellow-dot ball is used for most competitive matches. Other faster balls used on cold courts or by beginners have either white, red, or blue dots.

ABOUT THE AUTHOR

Philip Yarrow began competing in and winning squash tournaments as a member of the Under-19 Junior Squad in his native England. While attending Nottingham University, he was both the English Universities and British Universities Champion. His school's team won the English Universities Team Championship during his years there. While the U.S. National Amateur Champion in 1992 and 1993, Yarrow was also building one of the best squash programs in the country as head squash professional at Chicago's Lakeshore Athletic Club. He is recognized as one of the key figures in the recent switch by U.S. players from the North American hard-ball version to the international soft-ball version of the game.

Yarrow is an English Squash Rackets Association certified coach, an English- and U.S.-certified referee, and a U.S.-certified referee instructor. In addition to squash, the author also plays golf and chess. He lives in Oak Park, Illinois, with his wife, Virginia.

Sports Fundamentals Series

Learning sports basics has never been more effective—or more fun—than with the *Sports Fundamentals Series*. These books enable recreational athletes to engage in the activity quickly. Quick participation, not hours of reading, makes learning more fun and more effective.

Each chapter addresses a specific skill for that particular sport, leading the athlete through a simple, four-step sequence:

- *You Can Do It:* The skill is introduced with sequential instructions and accompanying photographs.
- *More to Choose and Use:* Variations and extensions of the primary skill are covered.
- *Take It to the Court/Field:* Readers learn how to apply the skill in competition.
- *Give It a Go:* These provide several direct experiences for gauging, developing, and honing the skill.

The writers of the *Sports Fundamentals Series* books are veteran instructors and coaches with extensive knowledge of their sport. They communicate clearly and succinctly, making reading and applying the content to the sport enjoyable for both younger and older recreational athletes. You're sure to get up to speed quickly on any sport you want to play.

The *Sports Fundamentals Series* includes:

- Archery
- Basketball
- Bowling
- Golf
- Racquetball
- Soccer
- Softball
- Tennis
- Volleyball
- Weight Training

HUMAN KINETICS
The Premier Publisher for Sports & Fitness
P.O. Box 5076, Champaign, IL 61825-5076
www.HumanKinetics.com

2335